✗

AUTHOR WHITTINGTON-
EGAN. R

TITLE
Liverpool soundings

CLASS No.
E O 2

BOOK No.
08559949

D0585763

LIVERPOOL SOUNDINGS

LIVERPOOL SOUNDINGS

BY

RICHARD WHITTINGTON-EGAN

THE GALLERY PRESS

08559949

L000273597
01900444

First published in this edition 1969
by The Gallery Press
Seel House, Seel Street,
Liverpool 1
© Richard Whittington-Egan

Printed by
Liverpool Letterpress Ltd.

This is my city,
And after the gusty gouts of rain
Have spread their silver scales
Over its wind-dusted pavements,
It is a clean, a silver city,
Where the picked bones of old civilizations
Whiten in the sea wind,
Like stark, black twigs
That winter crusts with ice-mould.

This is my city,
Where I walk in the wild wind on the hill brow.
And over the patchwork rooftops,
To a distant prospect of mountains,
The amber evening is snared, to linger on wet surfaces,
And mirrored in careless sea-shimmers,
Until the hunting night bears down across the riggings of
        the river-riding ships,
To drown it in the shadows of distance-looming hills.

CONTENTS

INTRODUCTION

Twelve, thirteen years ago, I wrote two books—*Liverpool Colonnade* and *Liverpool Roundabout*—in which I tried to capture something of the atmosphere of Liverpool. They were essentially a personal chronicle of the morning, noon and night town. A record of the many expressions that flit across the city's face—the bland, open countenance of her waterfront; the grey, furrowed visage of her industry; the smooth green acres of her parks and gardens; the bright twinkle of her pleasure haunts.

In those two books I told of the mystery, the tragedy and the romance that I found lying in waiting just around the corner of every street. And somehow, it seems, I must have succeeded in putting a flesh of words upon the skeletons of vague thoughts and feelings that danced in the hearts of others who, like myself, were hostages to the magic of Merseyside.

At any event, the editions were exhausted, and for some years now both volumes have been out of print, but not, happily, out of demand. Indeed, it is just because so many people still ask for them, that the Gallery Press has, in response to public demand, decided to reprint the present selection from them.

Nothing in life stands still. That is part of the sport and spilth of being alive. But the changes Time wreaks have their pathos. They mean that you can never, except in imagination, go back. To try to do so is to court disillusion—and find yourself wedded to despair. You can return, physically, to the old scenes. You can linger there nostalgically for a while, pretending to yourself that it is all just the same really. But you know that it is not. And, as the train bears you away, back to what life and the years have made you, you sadly realise that the make-believe is at last over. Perhaps that is what is meant by discovering that you are middle aged.

I remember a conversation I once had with a broken-down old boxer. Cauliflower-eared, more than a little punch-drunk, he had fought his way round the world. He could, perhaps, have been a success, but he neglected opportunities that might have led to fame and fortune because he could not bear to be far away from his native Liverpool. When I met him he was dying—and he knew it. He was living in a poor little house in a mean street. But he was utterly content. "I am back in Liverpool," he said wistfully, "and all my life, wherever in the world I went, I have been haunted by this dirty city on the banks of the Mersey."

I know exactly what he meant. For I, too, have been haunted by Liverpool. Haunted by the memory of delicately pale spring mornings among the rockeries and arbours of Prince's Park; long summer's evening strolls through Gateacre and Woolton, and beneath the trees of

Aigburth; brooding autumn tea-times when plumes of burning leaf smoke rose from the gardens of old Victorian streets and squares; winter nights, with the smell of Christmas in the air, and the mist creeping through the spider's web of streets that lie about the river.

The spectres of a thousand trivialities have risen to plague me, beckoning the more insistently because they are for ever irretrievably out of reach.

You see, the Liverpool that I lived in and wrote about exists now only in my memory. It has no location in space. I carry it around within the belfry of my skull. I cherish it because it *is* my youth. The reality is gone, alas, like my youth too soon.

That is why, here and there, you may find that some fact, some description, some observation, is slightly out of date, anchored to a specific moment in time, like a mammoth frozen into the ice of the past —or a fly preserved in the amber of an instant.

It would have been the easiest thing in the world to add a complement of subsequent changes and contemporary angles, but I have deliberately resisted the temptation. My whole intention was to present a portrait of one man's city as it existed in the mid-twentieth century.

To titivate it would have been to destroy it.

Nor, indeed, has my Liverpool all been washed away by the waters of the moon.

The Liver Birds have not flown.

Great George still ticks remorselessly on, measuring the minutes, and chiming away the hours of other people's youth.

The One O'Clock Gun still scatters its grey smoke-puff of pigeons.

The beer still foams cool and clear in the brown-varnished pubs.

The hammers still ring out on the bankers of Mount Zion.

The city lights still gleam as brightly.

And I doubt not that somewhere in the Liverpool of today some other youngster walks in my tracks, discovering for himself all those selfsame things that once I discovered with the selfsame delight.

I have summoned a bizarre company of actors from their limbo beyond the cemetery gates, to move once more across the shadowy Liverpool stage that saw their deaths and entrances . . .

I have gathered a garland of legends, woven a wreath of wraiths, compiled a sort of logbook of old romances . . .

And here it is, diffidently offered to the young man of today, by that young man of yesterday . . .

RICHARD WHITTINGTON-EGAN

COSSETING THE CALDER STONES

I have just been to the Cleansing Department Yard in Garston Old Road to see the earliest example of man's handiwork on Merseyside—some 4,000-year-old stone-carvings.

An official lifted the edge of a huge tarpaulin, and there, prone upon the cobbles, lay six great slabs of sandstone which have, for the last 109 years, stood at the entrance to Calderstones Park, marking the junction of three townships.

First mentioned in the year 1568, when they were cited as an undisputed boundary point during a territorial disagreement between the Manors of Allerton and Wavertree, the Calder Stones have been an enigma to the autochthonous Merseysider for close on 400 years. In mediæval times, an ignorant peasantry inclined to the view that they were somehow connected with witchcraft, a belief which may well have originated with the Saxons, for one interpretation of the complex etymology of the word *Calder* is that it stems from the Anglo-Saxon *Gualder* which means a wizard or warlock. This notion persisted for centuries, until, in fact, Stukeley and other disciples of romantic eighteenth-century antiquarian fervour initiated the cult of the Druid, when the Calder Stones came to be regarded as a " Druidical Circle," and queasy folk of archaeological bent professed to see in them a·sacrificial temple redolent of mistletoe, golden sickles and runnelled altar-stones disgustingly besmirched with the blood of human sacrifices ! A quaint conception enshrined to this day in the name of the nearby district of Druids Cross.

Informed twentieth-century opinion, derived from the painstaking researches of modern science, has substituted for this lurid legend a less bloody, though in no respect less wonderful, history, which has the additional advantage of accuracy.

The clue to the real nature of the Calder Stones is to be found in certain ancient records. In 1896, a local antiquary, E. W. Cox, related how his gardener, Robert Peers (1801-1887), who had worked on Calderstones Farm as a boy, remembered the stones being partially buried in a large mound of sand. From various sources it appears that although at one time only small portions of some of the stones were visible protruding from the top of this little hillock, between 1760 and 1790 much of the sand was carted away by builders. By

1805, the mound had been so severely diminished that it collapsed, and, in 1815, it was entirely removed when the road was widened. After that, the stones lay neglected on the farm until the illustrious William Roscoe of Allerton Hall had them set up in a " Druids' Circle." Subsequently, in 1845, the circle was enclosed, by the order of Joseph Need Walker of Calderstone House, within a low stone wall surmounted by stout railings. This planting of the stones in a ring was very misleading for it suggested that they had originally formed a cromlech—a kind of miniature Stonehenge. This was not so, for the evidence of early descriptions makes it abundantly clear that the Calder Stones made up a stone burial-chamber bedded in a tumulus of the type which present-day archaeologists call a barrow.

These barrows occur all over Britain and in many other parts of the world. The conspicuous manner in which they hug the coast-line from Land's End to Orkney, and cluster about inland waterways which connect with the sea, suggests that they are the work of a maritime people who made the Atlantic and the Irish Sea their high-ways. They are generally attributed to the Iberians, an advanced group of Mediterranean folk, ultimately deriving from Egypt, whose unity was one of strong religious tradition. Their religion has been termed *Megalithic* (Greek. Big Stone) because one of its chief tenets lay in the construction of big stone monuments, the vast majority of which were funerary in function.

In all Near East and Mediterranean centres of civilization—particularly in Egypt—vast labours and wealth were expended upon the dead in order to secure their contentment in the next world and, the cynic might hazard, to ensure their continued goodwill towards their survivors. In rocky districts inhumation in natural caves or rock-cut sepulchres was the custom ; where, however, no rock occurred, stone tombs had to be built. The pyramids themselves are nothing more than gigantic artificial caves. When, perhaps in search of *lebensraum*, the Iberians set out upon their migrations, they took their megalithic ideals with them and scattered innumerable examples of their Cyclopean architecture in their wake. All these, despite the emergence of several distinct traditions as a result of local schisms, display a sufficiently strict agreement in arbitrary detail to make them as reliable witnesses of megalithic religion as are mosques for Mohammedanism.

After about 2,500 B.C., men raised such monuments in Sicily, Sardinia, Southern France, Spain and Portugal. From these centres the practice extended to Brittany, to our own coasts and onwards to the shores of the Baltic, until, at the end of 500 years, the megaliths pointed like Gargantuan milestones the progress of the navigators in little dug-out canoes, past Gibraltar, across the Bay of Biscay and right up to Sweden.

The Calder Stones, which by the way were situated less than two miles in direct line from the coast, probably represent colonisation by Megalithic Iberians via Ireland, and belong to the same art tradition as the circular chambered-tomb of Bryn Celli Dhu at Anglesey and the cruciform chambered-tomb of Barclodiad y Gawres. All three were nothing more or less than carefully contrived mausoleums. They vary in structural details it is true, but architectural differences do not necessarily reflect differences in faith, for does not the tin Bethel preach the same gospel as the cruciform cathedral? Each barrow was built as a family vault to shelter the remains of a chief and those of the members of his family. The Megalithic burial-ritual seems to have been fairly complicated. In the British Isles cremation was the normal rite, and in the case of the Calder Stones the discovery of several coarse clay cinerary-urns containing quantities of calcined human bones, confirms its practice. It is easy to imagine the scene. A great chieftain was dead; he had passed into the land of his fathers. Amidst the wailings and lamentations of his people the hallowed corpse would be carried to some spot close to the grave it was to occupy. Perhaps a tall wooden funeral-pyre had been erected, and the body was placed reverently upon its summit. The high-priest or holy man of the tribe would then set the great pile alight and its flickering flames would soon flare up, consuming the corpse and silhouetting the queer, skin-clad figures of the mourners against the horizon. As the last flames died down, the charred bones would be gathered from the smouldering heap, scooped into a special urn, and, to the accompaniment of mystic chanting and incantations, be placed in the dark rock-cavern which had been prepared for them.

Upon the surfaces of the Calder Stones there occur certain carvings in the form of spirals, concentric circles and so-called cup-and-ring markings. Their significance is obscure, but they were probably religious symbols connected with the magical aspect of the burial-ritual and very likely disclose the chthonic deity to whose bosom the faithful dead hoped to return. In any event they are invaluable, numbering among the first important efforts at non-representational art in western Europe, and constituting the sole expression of serious decorative purpose prior to the advent of the beautiful secular art of the Celts nearly 2,000 years later. Moreover, they establish an informative link with the great Hibernian megalithic monument of New Grange, Co. Meath, Ireland, which is situated almost directly opposite Liverpool on the other side of the Irish Sea, and upon which identical markings are present.

It was concern for the fate of these carvings on the Calder Stones which, in November 1952, worried Mr. J. H. Iliffe, director of the Liverpool Museum. After carrying out an examination and test excavation, he said that the markings were deteriorating due to weather-erosion, and proposed that they should be removed from their exposed site on Menlove Avenue. Accordingly, one September morning in 1954, nine men with a mobile crane and a low-loader set about removing the stones. It was no easy task, for the largest stone weighed more than 3 tons and even the smallest was a burden of 4 or 5 cwt. However, the job was accomplished in a single day, and, carefully wrapped in sacking, the stones were transported to the Corporation Yard where they now lie.

I talked with Mr. J. L. Forde-Johnston, the archaeologist who is coping with the detailed examination of the stones. Sitting at his desk in a room in Carnatic Hall which was littered with dusty adzes and flints and looked, in the blood-orange light of the November afternoon sunshine, like a prehistoric armoury, he told me of his work on the Calder Stones. Apparently, the cleansing yard is an appropriate place for them, for the stones are in a very bad state. Even the atmosphere of Liverpool's green belt seems to be none too pure, for it has stained them as black as jet. Mr. Forde-Johnston had already set to work cleaning them with a toothbrush ! He had also begun to paint them with a green solution of latex rubber which takes very adequate impressions of the carvings. On a nearby work-table I saw a series of careful scale-drawings which were being completed and which will record for posterity all the markings, including any which may be discovered on portions of the stones hitherto buried in the ground.

The ultimate fate of the Calder Stones still hangs in the balance. Some people would like to see them housed under cover in the museum and artificial stone replicas erected at the entrance to Calderstones Park. But whatever decision is eventually reached, we may be sure that it will be to preserve Liverpool's 4,000-year-old heritage, for a wise committee of city fathers is well aware of their unique importance and is fully determined to cosset the Calder Stones.

A FORGOTTEN GARDEN

There were just the three of us in the garden that afternoon, myself, Tam O'Shanter and Souter Johnny. Perhaps the weather had something to do with it, for it was one of those dull, drizzly days with the sun hidden by that low-hanging curtain of cloud behind which it had been sulking practically all of that sullen summer.

Even in such dismal weather, the Botanic Garden was beautiful. Parterres studded with bed after bed of jewel-bright flowers and lawns of the greenest and most velvety grass bore witness to the care with which it was tended, and yet, inexplicably, an air of desolation hovered about the place. For fully half an hour I walked the winding paths which led past forlorn little gazebos, deserted arbours and lonely rockeries, without encountering another living soul. Then I made my way back along the broad main terrace, its huge Grecian urns overflowing with a scarlet foam of geraniums, to where, beside a lily-covered pool, Tam and Johnny sat gazing stonily across their desolate demesne.

In some curious way those two statues seem the petrified embodiment of the whole sorry story of decline which is the latter-day history of Liverpool's Botanic Garden. Sculptured by a self-taught artist, Mr. Thom, they represent two robust characters immortalised by Scotland's Rabbie Burns—Douglas Graham as Tam O' Shanter and John Davidson, the shoemaker, as Souter Johnny. They first came to Liverpool in 1830, when they were exhibited at 26 Church Street, where thousands of people paid a shilling for the privilege of viewing them. Standing there alone beside them in the soft drizzle which had begun to fall, I found it difficult to realise that these neglected figures had once been visited and " their merits highly appreciated " by no less a person than George IV and that during their exhibition in London upwards of 80,000 people had flocked to see them. Now, Tam, his nose broken by local hooligans, and Johnny, his right arm long since lost, linger on sufferance, for, round about 1908 they were removed and it was only at the earnest request of the local Burns Club that they were reinstated in that little corner of Liverpool which they still grace. They, like the Botanic Garden itself, have seen better days and they, like it, seem wrapped in memories of a more splendid past.

As I made my way past the brown stretch of barren earth which marks like a scar the spot where once the lofty palmhouse and its attendant pavilions of glass rose sparkling to the sky, I remembered the splendours which used to be housed there. Entering that great hothouse you were, in an instant, transported from the cold, smoke-stained air of Liverpool into the warm, perfumed atmosphere of kinder climes. And all about you bloomed a lush jungle of exotic plant life. There were the palms, the yams, the banana-trees, the clumps of sugar-cane, the coffee-bushes and the fascinatingly named dragon's-blood-tree ; specimens of vanilla-plants, bottle-gourds, loofahs and the papyrus-plant, from which the ancients made their paper. There, too, you could inspect the cotton-plant, to which Liverpool owes so much of its prosperity. There was even a grove of miniature orange-trees, whilst a magnificent display of orchids and an extensive collection of carnivorous plants, which you could watch as they caught and ate insects, were always great attractions. But now these delights are no more, dispersed, like so many other things, by a German bomb.

It was as I was leaving the garden that I noticed the railings, or rather the lack of them. This is, of course, another legacy of the war, but their continued absence emphasised for me, as nothing else could, the tremendous change which has, over the years, taken place in the public's attitude to the Botanic Garden. There was no lack of railings 151 years ago when it was first opened. Indeed, in those days of the flood-tide of enthusiasm, the garden was a very exclusive place, admission to which was strictly limited to the proprietors and their friends, a fact which many people bitterly resented. Now, in the Age of the Common Man, when the barriers have been swept aside and it is open to all, hardly anyone bothers to visit it.

Actually, the first Botanic Garden was founded and owned by a private company. In the year 1800 a group of Liverpool botanists and nature-lovers, headed by that most famous son of Liverpool, William Roscoe, banded together and decided to form a botanic garden. The idea was then a novel one, for such gardens as existed at that time were for the most part Physic Gardens, established solely for the purpose of cultivating medicinal plants and herbs. Roscoe and his friends acquired five acres of land in an area of open country at the top of Mount Pleasant known as Mosslake Fields. This they enclosed and laid out with numerous beds of flowers, trees, bushes and shrubs. They also constructed an enormous conservatory wherein flourished tropic palms, graceful ferns and many a rare plant brought home to Liverpool from the four corners of the earth by ships' masters who cherished a taste for botany. By all accounts, the Botanic Garden, which first opened its gates in 1803, was a charming place, a favourite rendezvous of the cream of Liverpool society, where ladies and gentlemen, clad in silks and satins that bade fair to rival the flowers themselves in hue, would walk on long summer evenings while a band played gently among the trees. But it was far from being only a pleasure-resort. Under the administration of its first curator, John Shepherd, the garden became a famous centre of botanical study thirty-eight years before London's Kew Gardens came into existence. Its fame spread abroad. Philadelphia set to work to construct a garden on the Liverpool principle : Calcutta sent an order for a number of special fruit-trees and even Russia was sufficiently impressed to establish a similar garden in Leningrad—then St. Petersburg. Moreover, the Emperor of Russia procured vast quantities of plants from Liverpool with which to stock his Imperial Botanic Gardens, and, in 1826, Shepherd was invited to the Russian Embassy in London where he was presented with a diamond ring, Czar Alexander's personal gift of gratitude for his services to Russian botanical science.

Shepherd died in 1836 and in that same year it was decided that because of the rapid extension of the town, which had already entirely surrounded it with buildings, the garden should be removed to Edge Lane. The site of the first Botanic Garden, a roughly triangular area bounded by Myrtle Street, Olive Street and Melville Place, was soon lost beneath the foundations of new houses and today its whilom presence is commemorated only by a fragrant bouquet of street names —Almond, Date, Ivy, Laurel, Mulberry, Vine, Palm and Walnut Streets, along whose stone-carpeted lengths scarcely a single blade of green grass pushes through.

In its new location of $11\frac{1}{4}$ acres, the second Botanic Garden continued for the next five years as exclusive as its predecessor, but, in 1841, it was taken over by the Liverpool Corporation and thrown open to the public.

Throughout the remainder of the nineteenth-century and well into the present one, the garden prospered, but by 1936 public interest in it had waned. The Housing Committee proposed that it should be done away with and the land used for the erection of corporation houses, but this suggestion led to such a chorus of protest that the idea was dropped. Despite this brief flare-up of concern for its welfare, the garden continued to decline. In 1937 the aviary was demolished. During the Second World War the glasshouses were shattered by bombs, and by 1946 it was being generally acknowledged that the old garden was " doomed to gradual extinction."

Six years ago the Liverpool Parks and Gardens Committee finally determined that the garden would have to be dismantled and its site made into a model traffic-area, a kind of School for Safety, similar to that which exists at Tottenham, where children could be taught the rules of road-sense in an all-out effort to reduce the awful toll of street accidents.

Today, that plan is being put into action and those who wish to pay a last visit to what was once described as the most beautiful park in England had best not put it off too long or they will find instead a place laid out with traffic-lights and zebra-crossings, where children whizz around on fairy-cycles, and, if present proposals are approved, beside which, helicopters will drop to earth upon a new, circular landing-ground.

I spoke to Mr. P. W. H. Conn, Chief-Superintendent of Parks and Gardens, about these impending changes. " Liverpool is not losing its Botanic Garden," he told me, " it is simply that its third one is being opened at Calderstones where we intend to restore it to its former glory. For many years now the smoky atmosphere of Edge Lane has proved unsuitable for the purpose." I have no doubt that the third Botanic Garden will eventually be the finest that Liverpool has ever seen, but, along with many more sentimental people, I cannot help feeling a sneaking regret at the passing of one of the very first " lungs " of this city and casting an affectionate glance back to the days when, for more than a century, you could be sure of finding palms and papyrus growing in Edge Lane.

IRON HORSES OF LIVERPOOL

Below the modern level of a busy main street, within a stone's throw of the first great passenger railway station in the world, a sloping, grass-banked ramp leads you to Liverpool's "ghost" station.

Here, in a small, subterranean-seeming corner of Edge Lane, something of time has been preserved. The years, aided by the ever-willing destructiveness of human hands, have wrought sad havoc upon the mouldering masonry of Edge Lane Station. Deserted platforms stretch below the broken back-crest of its buildings, over which a green river of weeds has poured, and the strangling bindweed has set its grip about all within its reach. Yet from this chaos, it is possible to re-create a vanishing type of station still to be glimpsed in out-of-the-way places around which the tide of modernity has advanced, leaving, as it were, a spit of sand temporarily untouched.

How well one knows them, these picturesque chance survivals, with their singing gas-jets imprisoned in crystal cages, supported on the summits of ornate ironwork brackets and columns : with their rusting tin advertisements for Mazawattee Tea, to charm the dusted throats of generations of thirsty travellers, and Iron Jelloids and Owbridges' Lung Tonic to insinuate themselves into travel-weary minds at just that psychological moment when fatigued bodies are peculiarly susceptible to the promise of patent panaceas! And there, too, is the compelling blue splotch of Stephens' Ink, sullying interminably the white enamel expanse, like some half-remembered page of childhood's blotted copy-book.

But, at Edge Lane, these things are merely ghosts, and, standing amidst the rubble of spilled bricks and splintered woodwork, seeing the bare booking-office and the dead waiting-room, where shadows wait for the train that will never come, one feels the span of years diminish. And if the empty rafters were suddenly to resound to the asthma of some tall-stacked, spiky-wheeled locomotive of a hundred years ago, it could evoke nothing of surprise. It is as if that barren waiting-room is become an ante-room to the past and the mind travels back to the cradle days of our English railways and hovers awhile about the fascinating saga of the iron road.

Although the commencement of the Railway Age does not extend further into antiquity than the early years of the nineteenth-century, if we are to trace the evolutionary line along which its trains were borne, it will be necessary for us to go back several hundred years. In the days when Charles II was occupying the throne, the main problem with which the English collieries had to contend was that of transporting coal from the pit-head to the nearest port, whence it was carried by coasters to those localities where it was required. Originally, it was the custom to employ large numbers of horse-drawn trucks for this purpose, and the need for smooth haulage roads was supplied by the laying down of a series of wooden planks along which the chaldron wheels could pass unimpeded. But wood was far from satisfactory, in that it soon wore out, and by the eighteenth-century it had become the practice to lay iron plates over the wood.

It was not, however, until 1776 that an all-iron rail-way was built near Sheffield, and the rails provided with an inside flange to prevent wheel slip. Thus early, we discover that rail-ways existed long before the trains which we have come to associate with them.

With Watt's invention of the separate steam-condenser at the end of the eighteenth-century, a new era was initiated. Intensive mechanisation was the order of the day and the rapidly expanding volume of commodities resulting from the new, steam-speeded industries made it clear that something in the nature of a transport revolution had become necessary. The first efforts to this end had begun with the construction of a canal between Manchester and the Duke of Bridgewater's colliery at Worsley in 1760, but with the harnessing of steam-power, new possibilities were envisaged.

In the year 1786, William Murdock, a Scottish engineer then employed in Cornwall, invented the first engine to run on wheels— the first locomotive engine. Trying it out one night in a local country lane, he is reputed to have frightened the local parson into thinking that he had seen the devil !

But the title of " Father of the Locomotive " has been bestowed upon Richard Trevithick, who built his first locomotive in 1801. In 1803, Trevithick actually took his engine to London, where it caused a tremendous stir as it chugged through the streets. Encouraged by his success, Trevithick paid a second visit to London in 1808. This time he turned his engine to financial benefit by setting it up on a circular, iron track near Euston Square and giving people rides at five shillings a trip. Meanwhile, in 1804, a rack engine of Trevithick's design was put to work on the old colliery plate-way at Merthyr Tydfil.

In 1815, George Stephenson, the one-time pit-boy and son of a labourer who was eighteen before he learned to read and write, invented a locomotive, which he built and named the *Blucher*. Stephenson had always considered that horse-traction was a slow and uneconomical method of coal-haulage, and his idea that steam-engines, designed to run on rail-ways, would be more suited to the task was amply confirmed at Killingworth colliery, where his *Blucher* successfully hauled trucks of coal some nine miles to the coast.

The first real progress in the direction of that vast metamorphosis which was to ring Britain with iron roads and finally reduce the time and hazards of travel, came in 1825 with the opening of a passenger railway between Stockton and Darlington. This line had been laid down under the direction of Stephenson and it was while he was engaged in its construction that he was approached by a newly-organised company with a proposal that he should undertake the laying down of a line between Liverpool and Manchester.

For some time, both Liverpool and Manchester merchants had been seriously dissatisfied with the delays and high charges of road, river and canal transport between their two towns. The Liverpool corn merchants in particular were outraged by prevailing conditions, and it was largely at their instigation that the possibility of a railway came to be considered.

To propose was one thing ; to actually build the railway was another matter. First of all there were the landowners to contend with. Many of them, quite understandably, did not want a railway line cutting across their estates. All manner of scenes took place between the surveyors and irate landlords. At one stage things got so bad that the surveyors had to hire a bodyguard to protect them from physical injury at the hands of a pugilistically inclined miner from St. Helens. There were also legislative difficulties. Before the line could be laid Parliamentary consent had to be secured. M.P. land-owners and their friends voted against the proposal and it was rejected. Re-introduced in 1826, it was approved and work started in earnest.

The laying of the Liverpool-Manchester line was a gigantic undertaking, in the course of which innumerable tunnels had to be driven, cuttings made, hollows filled in and sixty-three bridges and viaducts erected. But the worst problem of all was Chat Moss, a ten-mile square tract of bog-land, some forty feet deep in places, which lay between Worsley, Glazebrook and Leigh. Everything laid upon it promptly sank into the morass. Stephenson eventually decided to " float " his line across it, by distributing the load over a wide surface, specially prepared by laying sand, earth and gravel, thickly coated with cinders, upon overlapping hurdles of branches, heather and brushwood.

Nor was it entirely plain sailing even when the line was at last finished, for there was a difference of opinion as to whether loco-motive or stationary engines (with drums and coils) would be the more satisfactory. It was finally decided to hold a competition in order to test the capabilities of locomotives. A prize of £500 was offered, and five locomotives were entered for what came to be known as the Rainhill trials. It is a matter of history that George Stephenson's *Rocket* achieved an easy victory, drawing a load of practically three times its own weight at a speed of nearly 14 miles an hour, thus settling the question of the future locomotion of the world.

At last, on Wednesday, 15th September, 1830, all was ready for the official opening of the Liverpool and Manchester Railway and, upon a glorious autumn morning, crowds of some fifty-thousand people made their way to the terminus at Edge Hill to see the inauguration of the £820,000 venture. The ceremony was performed by the Duke of Wellington. The Duke entered a magnificent carriage (specially prepared for the occasion) linked to which were two other coaches containing a brilliant assemblage of notables, and a third coach occupied by a band, the whole being drawn by Stephenson's *Northumbrian*, with Stephenson himself on the footplate. At 10-40 a.m. the procession of eight trains, fluttering gaily their colourful drapery of flags and bunting, moved slowly off, to the accompaniment of tumultuous cheering and the strains of the band.

All along the thirty miles of its course the route was lined with enthusiastic spectators, many of whom were accommodated in specially-erected grandstands. Everything went according to plan until the procession came to Parkside, near Kenyon, where the engines were uncoupled to take in water. Here many passengers alighted and crossed the line in order to chatter with their friends. Among these was William Huskisson, the famous M.P. for Liverpool, who had but recently left his sick-bed in order to be present at the historic occasion. Seeing the Duke, and anxious to grasp the opportunity of making up a quarrel which he had had with him in the previous October, Huskisson hurried towards His Grace's coach. Suddenly a locomotive was seen approaching and the cry was raised, " Take care, an engine is coming ! " There was a general rush, in the course of which Huskisson slipped and fell on the line in the path of the *Rocket* which passed over his leg, fracturing it in two places. He was immediately hoisted aboard the *Rocket* and taken to Eccles Vicarage, but the shock must have been too great for him in his weakened state, for at nine o'clock that same evening, he died.

This unfortunate accident cast a gloom over the remainder of that memorable day, but from then onwards nothing was to stem the fantastically rapid progress of the iron road. Indeed, so great was the success of the railways of the 'thirties, that there arose a mania for speculating in such rolling-stock. At the climax of the speculative fever of 1845, the " Railway King," George Hudson, secured within two days the approval of thousands of shareholders for schemes involving an expenditure of ten million pounds. The direct result of all this over-speculation was the terrible slump of 1847-8 with its consequent ruin of thousands. At the end of the first year of Queen Victoria's reign there were barely 200 miles of railway lines in this country. By 1851 the total mileage had risen to about 7,000, while today there are more than 25,000 miles of track in Great Britain and nearly 750,000 miles of it throughout the world.

For six years after the opening of the Liverpool and Manchester line passengers were taken by horse-bus to the Edge Hill terminus.

During that time Stephenson and his workmen were busy hewing their way through solid rock to Lime Street. One day a gang of Irish navvies—the name is a relic of the old navigational-canal-building days when the labourers were thus known—engaged upon the making of the Lime Street tunnel were thoroughly alarmed to hear strange noises proceeding from the rock beneath their feet. Suddenly, one of their picks went right through the floor and from the resultant hole there emerged an enraged human head. The workmen fled in mortal terror. They did not know that they were trespassing upon the subterranean preserves of the redoubtable Joseph Williamson . . . but that is another story ! The tunnel proceeded without further incident and, in 1836, Lime Street Station was opened.

We have come a long way since those dream-distant days when the first iron horses careered at the wild speed of thirty miles an hour along their bright new rails, but here and there the observant eye can still perceive relics of Liverpool's railway revolution. In Tunnel Road we discover the Tunnel Hotel which was built in 1840 and whither passengers were borne in omnibuses from the Town Hall eight times daily, and where the intending traveller could be sure of " suitable refreshments and every comfort and accommodation being in constant readiness." Further out, at Broadgreen, the name of the present Rocket Hotel commemorates the coming of Stephenson's wonderful old locomotive to the district. The original long, low, straw-thatched cottage which was the first Rocket Inn, is alas, no longer in existence. But all of this neighbourhood seems charged with memories of an eventful past. Close by the old Broadgreen station, which stood near the original Rocket Inn, was George Cunningham's famous nursery and here he and George Stephenson had many a serious talk about the anticipated effect of the smoke and vibration of the latter's trains upon the former's plants. The two Georges became firm friends and George Cunningham it was who, when Stephenson's railway was formally opened, decorated the nearby bridge with thousands of his scarlet dahlias, then quite a new flower in this country, making a display which drew from *The Times* an enthusiastic comment upon the magnificence of the spectacle.

Proud, then, can the citizen of Liverpool be of the part which his city has played in the drama of the iron road and wheresoever in the world the path of necessity may take him, the sight or sound of a train should flee his mind back to that corner of south-west Lancashire where lies the city which is his birthright.

ROMANCE OF A CEMETERY

I have just been taking the waters at the Liverpool Spa.. The flat, slightly iron-tainted taste of the ice-cold water is still on my tongue, and although, mercifully, I do not suffer from rheumatism, I understand that the spa water used to be regarded as " tending to the cure of rheumatic complaints."

Actually, the Spa is a chalybeate spring which flows from the rock at the base of the cliff-like wall which lines the eastern side of St. James's Cemetery. It first came into prominence in 1773 when James Worthington, a Liverpool surgeon, published a small tract recommending its use in cases of loss of appetite, nerve disorders, lowness of spirits, headaches " proceeding from crudities of the stomach," rickets and weak eyes. A little later in that same year, another Liverpool physician, Dr. Thomas Houlston, wrote a more ambitious pamphlet belauding the virtues of the mineral spring and subsequently made a communication on the subject to the Royal Society. Though never styled " holy," the spring continued in great esteem, principally for the cure of diseases of the eye, for more than a century, and I have been told by an old inhabitant of Liverpool that he could remember the time when hundreds of people would come from all over Lancashire and wait in line with small bottles to take away some of the precious liquid. Latterly, however, the Liverpool Spa seems to have fallen into disrepute and there are very few visitors to the spot where, beneath the pious inscription :

> *Christian reader view in me,*
> *An emblem of true charity,*
> *Who freely what I have bestow,*
> *Though neither heard nor seen to flow,*
> *And I have full returns from Heaven,*
> *For every cup of water given.*

the mirifical spring still spills unceasingly into its worn stone basin.

At the time of the spring's discovery, the site of St. James's Cemetery was a quarry which had for countless years supplied sand-stone for building purposes. Many of Liverpool's ancient buildings, including the Town Hall, the old Corn Exchange, St. Thomas's, St. Paul's and St. John's churches, were constructed of stone hewn from it. By 1825 the quarry had become exhausted and the Corporation, to whom it belonged, had to find an answer to the awkward question of what to do with the extensive excavation which lay like a Brobdingnagian wound in the heart of the town. Too immense to be easily filled in, it was at first proposed to convert its ten neglected acres into a public garden. It was just about this time, however, that the Middlesex authorities, faced with a similar problem, decided to utilise a disused quarry at Kensal Green as a cemetery, and the Liverpool city fathers gave their approval to the formation of a company which undertook the conversion of the quarry to a burying-ground. So it was, in the February of 1825, that a new cemetery in connection with the Established Church, and named after St. James's Church, Toxteth Park, was commenced. The cemetery was consecrated in 1829 and the first interment took place to the accompaniment of one of the worst thunderstorms of the century on June 11th of that year. Since then there have been some 57,774 interments, the last of which was on July 10th, 1936, and now the old burial-ground is full.

Standing in the midst of this vast stone forest of memory, the eye is bewildered by its crowded profusion of tombstones. A little exploration is rewarded, however, by the discovery of some extremely interesting graves. Here you will find for instance, a tablet commemorating Sarah Biffin who, though born in 1784 without either arms or hands, contrived to become one of the most noted artists of her day. She worked with a long-handled brush, one end of which was secured beneath a pin or loop on her right shoulder, and the other she manipulated with her mouth. Her work was patronised by four British Monarchs—George III, George IV, William IV and Queen Victoria—and such was her fame that she is even referred to by Charles Dickens in Chapter 37 of *Nicholas Nickleby* and Chapter 28 of *Martin Chuzzlewit*. In later life she fell into great poverty but, befriended by Richard Rathbone, she ended her days in comparative comfort. She died at Number 8 Duke Street on October 2nd, 1850. Here, too, is the tomb of William Lynn, landlord of the Waterloo Hotel at Aintree ; the man who may be said to have initiated the Grand National when, in 1836, he persuaded his farmer neighbours to permit an annual Liverpool Steeplechase to be run over their land at Maghull. And all about you are the graves of sailors and master-mariners who, after lives spent on the tossing oceans of the world, have found a final harbour deep in the still heart of this peaceful corner of Sailor Town. Among them lies Captain John Oliver, veteran of the Battles of the Nile, Copenhagen, and Trafalgar, in which latter he served under Lord Nelson on H.M.S. *Victory*. He died in 1876 at the advanced age of 102. And here, too, rests Captain William Harrison, who commanded the *Great Eastern*—the Great Iron Ship.

Scarcely had the new cemetery opened its gates when, in September 1830, one of its most distinguished sleepers was laid to rest in this quiet dormitory of the dead. This man was the Right Honourable

William Huskisson, M.P. for Liverpool, who had the dubious distinction of being killed by Stephenson's first engine—the *Rocket*. His tomb is that small, domed, circular temple which dominates the centre of the cemetery and is its grandest monument. He rests within beneath a fine marble statue of himself executed by John Gibson, R.A.

I could not help contrasting the lonely grandeur of Huskisson's magnificent mausoleum with the humble stone which, amidst a cluster of indistinguished graves, marks the spot where lies all that was mortal of Catherine Wilkinson. Of less exalted rank in life, Kitty Wilkinson is every bit as much a Liverpool immortal as William Huskisson, and while the mountain of laurel wreaths has long since withered and mouldered away from the politician's bleak, locked temple, I found on Kitty Wilkinson's grave a beer bottle from the narrow brown neck of which sprouted a gay little posy of wild flowers. It was a tribute which she would have loved. This Kitty Wilkinson was a remarkable woman but it is mainly on account of her work during the dreadful cholera epidemic of 1832 that she is remembered. Apart from fearlessly nursing the sick and dying, she threw open the tiny kitchen of her own home so that people could use her boiler to wash the infection from their disease-laden clothing. Ten years later, the first public establishment of baths and wash-houses in this country was opened in Upper Frederick Street and Kitty Wilkinson and her husband were put in charge of the place which had come into being as the direct result of an idea that had been born in their own kitchen.

Walking through the cemetery, one sees here and there a broken cross, an urn toppled from its pedestal, a gruesomely decapitated angel. This damage is not so much the result of the passage of the years as the work of teenage hooligans who scale the inadequate wire-fencing at night and amuse themselves by hurling stones at the monuments. But there are other and less violent changes. The lichen has crept over old tombstones and smoke has mellowed their pristine whiteness to a sort of charcoal grey. Weather has softened corners which, like sharp-angled sorrows, have grown less acute with time. The snows and rains of the years have blunted the deeply-incised anguish of epitaphs until they have become blurred as old memories. And yet the hand which has erased so much extolling of virtues has left clear a terrible indictment. Upon the tall headstone of Sydney Evans, wife of John Evans, solicitor of Carnarvon, who died, aged 71, on May Day, 1833, is engraved the sorry story of a mother's pain :

" By her express desire it is stated on her tomb that she was the affectionate mother of a son whose unparalleled wrongs and persecution in Carnarvon, Carnarvonshire, Liverpool, Lancashire, perpetrated, brought her old age oppressed with sorrow to the grave."

There it is, an accusing finger perpetually pointing from the coffin. It is as if the sorrowing mother would pursue her errant son beyond the death-bed. All those wrongs happened so very long ago, and yet their graven record cries out across the years like an unquiet voice from the grave.

And everywhere is evidenced a gentler neglect. The shining ivy twines about its sculpted image and nature has drawn a kindly green coverlet of tall grass over many little mounds. It is well, for this neglect has brought a wild beauty in its wake. Although it is a valley of the shadow of death, upon a sunny day St. James's Cemetery does not strike one in that way. It seems rather, a little oasis of fresh green life in the stony bosom of the hill, where bright butterflies flit about in the warm sunshine and birds sing lustily in the sanctuary which has been provided for them there. It is a place to equal the lovely cemetery at Constantinople with its Piranesi-like walls pierced by tiers of catacombs, its sloping ramps, down which great hearses of the past lumbered, drawn by gleaming horses with tossing black ostrich plumes, and the beautiful little mortuary chapel, a perfect miniature Greek temple, standing darkly upon its escarpment in wonderful contrast with the flushed face of the new cathedral. Today, its surface no longer broken by the sexton's spade, the old burying-ground lies tranquil. It is a haunt of ancient peace and on long summer evenings it is the chosen rendezvous of youth and age. The children play among the tombstones ; the old men sit and smoke their pipes, and if they think of death in these placid surroundings it is as a friend who comes with the soft-scented dusk to soothe tired eyes and gently close them in a long, long sleep.

CITY LIGHTS

We met at the Lark Lane " Muster " a quarter of an hour before the November dusk had drowned the last colour from the russet-tinted streets. You enter the Mustering Station through what seems like a hole in the wall and step into a small gaslit snug which is the cabined remnant of an earlier age. The foreman sits at a high wooden desk— straight from the pages of Dickens—surrounded by all the paraphernalia of the lamplighter's calling. One by one, the muffled figures of Liverpool's last Leeries slip in from the indigo twilight, to sign the duty book, shoulder their neat little ladders and disappear again like ghosts into the gathering night.

Christened by Robert Louis Stevenson " Leerie,"—

> For we are very lucky with a lamp before the door,
> And Leerie stops to light it as he lights so many more ;
> And O! before you hurry by with ladder and with light,
> O Leerie, see a little child and nod to him to-night.

the lamplighter is a rapidly vanishing figure of the Liverpool streets. Once, he walked the windy town, in his hand a mysterious long pole whose faintest touch brought golden light, and left his wake a glow-worm track of glistering radiance. Nowadays, he is called a Public Lamp Attendant, and time-clock mechanisms which, ticking eerily away in silent streets, automatically light and extinguish the lamps, have, since their introduction round about 1905, plucked the golden rod from Leerie's hand. His firefly trail has become a duller path of duty, a mere visit to each of his lank charges, to wind or set its clock, to clean or put things right when the street-lamp pops and sputters in mechanic rebellion.

The earliest record of any attempt to lighten the darkness of Liverpool dates back to December 10th, 1653, when the Council ordered that " twoe Lanthornes with twoe candles burning everie night in ye dark moone be sett out at the High Crosse (at the corner of Castle and Dale Streets) and at Whyte Crosse (at the corner of Tithebarn and Oldhall Streets), and places prepared to sett them in, everie night till past 8 of ye clock by ye Sarjant and Water Ballive. This to be observed from All Saints' to Candlemas."

Twenty years later, the Council hit upon an ingenious plan to improve a primitive street-lighting, which was dependent upon the

28

vagaries of guttering candles, without involving the burgesses in considerable expense. In the October of 1673 they accordingly resolved : " That every publick-house hang out Lanthornes and light candles at theire doors from the first of November next till the second of February next, till 8 of the clock at night from day shutting, upon penalty of VId a night." This was probably the origin of public-house lamps which were a constant feature until recent times.

In the year 1718, the first Liverpool Leerie came into being. His name was James Halsall and he undertook to attend, keep in order and light every night " for tenn shillings a piece per annum " forty-five oil-lamps with which the Council made brave effort to dispel the Stygian gloom. This eighteenth-century attempt at street-lighting was, however, far from successful, and the gentry would always take their own lighting with them. This entailed the employment of linkmen. The links were stiff lengths of tarred rope, about as thick as a man's arm, which yielded a poor, flaring light and vast quantities of horrid, bituminous smoke. Link-extinguishers, narrow iron funnels into which the flaming torch was plunged, used to be attached to lamp-irons. The better class houses always had lamp-irons attached either to their gates or railings or else above their doors. Some still survive in Rodney and Chatham Streets. Middle-class folk carried hand lanterns, while poor people just butted into one another and, every so often, walked clean into the Old Dock ! Only the footpads viewed such conditions with equanimity.

Towards the end of the eighteenth-century, a wily Scot, named William Murdock, experimenting with coal-gas, succeeded in lighting his office at Redruth, Cornwall, by its agency and, in 1803, he installed the first commercial gas-making and lighting plant at Boulton and Watt's works at Birmingham. It was the dawn of a bright new era.

One January night in 1816, the people of Liverpool were startled by the exhibition of two brilliant gas-lamps outside the Town Hall, and during the following year the first domiciliary gas-jets flared in the parlours of those who could afford such a luxury. In the circumstances, it is surprising to learn that, instead of being grateful for the new invention, an unlighted and unenlightened public grumbled un-ceasingly because the newly-formed Liverpool Gas Company was pulling up the streets to put down pipes for the distribution of the gas which was widely and contemptuously dubbed a " faddist's fluid." But whether they liked it or no, gas had come to stay, and, on September 11th, 1819, 30 gas-lamps cast their soft radiance over the Liverpool streets for the first time, and by the end of the year, 199 more gas-lamps had been erected in the town. Today, 11,013 gas-lamps still flee the shadows of Liverpool, but they are in process of being replaced by electricity.

Electricity was the force which was to deal the death-blow to the gas-lamp. Back in 1884, the first tentative experiments were being made with its power in the form of arc-lamps, but they were abandoned when the contractors went into liquidation. In the arc-lamp a very brilliant light is produced by passing an electric current across a small gap between two carbon rods, and in 1896 Bold Street was lit by a number of these arc-lamps suspended across the centre of the road. Elsewhere in the city, Brockie-Pell arc-lamps, placed on tall columns and fed from underground mains, were brought into use. The searching eye can still discover many of the old arc-lamp carriers in Parker Street, London Road, Catharine Street and various other places. But it was only in 1921, at which time little more than 10 miles of streets were electrically lit, when the greater density of traffic necessitated sharper night vision, that serious attention was given to the subject, with the result that within fifteen years practically 386 miles of streets had been electrified.

There are currently some 23,114 electric-lamps in commission in Liverpool, served by perhaps 3,000 miles of cable and using approximately 92,821 new bulbs every year. With an ever-increasing total of 34,127 light-points, illumining 892 miles of streets at an annual cost of something like £241,000, Liverpool is well in the running to become one of the best lit cities in the kingdom. The whole of this vast enterprise is administered by the City Lighting Department which employs 400 men under the able captaincy of Mr. C. C. Smith.

Moreover, our city has been a pioneer in the matter of street-lighting, for, in 1934, it was the birthplace of the amber way of the sodium anti-dazzle system which has played so vital a part in the reduction of the morbid figures of accident incidence. More recently, in 1953, there were installed at the Pier Head—Gateway to Liverpool—the first vertical cold cathode fluorescent lanterns in the country, probably in the world. A variation of this system, the warm cathode installation, has been introduced on Otterspool Promenade.

Constant headache to the men who keep the lamps of Liverpool burning, is that of vandalism. In 1953-4 alone, the bill for malicious damage totalled £3,736 of ratepayers' money. Important financial consideration as this undoubtedly is, it pales into insignificance beside the yardstick of awful consequences, in terms of accidents and human life, which the extinction of a single vitally-positioned light implies. Indeed, so serious had the state of affairs become in 1951, that the Corporation Lighting Committee went to the expense of making a three-minute film, appropriately titled, in Kiplingesian terms, "The Light that Failed." This film told, in the graphic manner of our pictorial age, the story of two senseless disasters resulting from heedless hooliganism, and its message was driven home by a vivid commentary from the lips of Liverpool's apostle of light, Alderman Alexander Critchley. In October 1950, following the battering to death of a woman on a blitzed-site in Great Newton Street, that thoroughfare became a street of frightened women because its pitch-black length

30

had not a single lamp alight. They had all been put out of action by louts.

It is only to be expected that among Liverpool's 34,000 lights, there should be several of especial interest. One dark night recently, I set out on a pilgrimage of light. The first lamp which I visited was not there ! But I gazed at the site, outside the Gaumont Cinema, Prince's Park, where it once stood, with something akin to reverence, for it was clinging to its vanished standard that, one April day in 1888, the great Victorian poet, Matthew Arnold, died.

From there I made my way to Wolstenholme Square. In the centre of that cobbled quadrant towers a mammoth lamp-post which has for its base the plinth of a long-demolished sundial; a forlorn relic of the days when this ancient square was a sequestered place of green lawns and sheltered elms, and fair ladies were embowered behind the muslin curtains of drawing-rooms which are since become dingy warehouse offices.

The third of my objectives was a lamp unique in Liverpool, for it is one which remains alight throughout the daylight hours and is extinguished at nightfall. It is situated actually INSIDE an office-building in Sweeting Street, where it illumines the dark recesses of a gloomy passage. At day's end, when the building is closed and its office staffs are snugly bedded in the dormitories of suburbia, its needless light is doused.

By the time I reached Brunswick Square, the last port of call in my lamp-hunt, the fog which had threatened all evening was unrolling its great vaporous blanket about the north end of the town. Nevertheless, I had little difficulty in discerning " the monument " which loomed bulkishly out of the mist. This tall, square pillar of stone is indeed a monument, recalling as it does the dark days in Liverpool. In actual fact, it is a lamp-post of an unusual sort, and in olden times an oil-lamp used to burn upon the flat platform of its crest. The lamplighter who tended its beacon was a woman, and as recently as 1930, her 75-year-old daughter still lived in the square. Strangely enough, Liverpool's early oil-lamps were mostly kept in trim by women, and one which stood in Wavertree Nook within living memory was constantly tended by a lady of the lamp. Liverpool's last oil-lamp, a more conventional affair resembling an ordinary gas-lamp, burned right up to the beginning of the Second World War. A solitary anachronism, sited at Orient Drive, Gateacre, it was consigned to the care of the late Mr. Bill Williamson, forty years a Liverpool Leerie.

And what of the future ? City Lighting Engineer, Mr. C. C. Smith dreams of a Liverpool " lit by fewer lamps of higher power and at greater mounting heights."

We have come a long way since that distant December night, when the Council made its first attempt to dispel the gloom of certain

31

of the town's chief thoroughfares.   Candles, oil and gas have come and gone, and "Leerie" himself is almost an anachronism.   And with him is departed childhood's old delight of watching his slender wand coax the black stems of the street-lamps into golden flower.   Now, with the sharp click of a switch, whole streets are electrically and un-romantically illuminated.   Even the rakishly top-hatted gas-lamps are giving way to tall, concrete-columned utility, and progress postulates sodium and, *par excellence*, cold cathode, lighting, where once the gentle singing gas did softer battle with the dark.

Very soon now, the brilliant rays of the new lamps of Liverpool will have dissolved for ever the romantic shadow of the lamplighter. He will have gone to join the muffin-man, with whom he shared so many twilit afternoons in the long-ago, in the misty niches of old memories. He will have become a wraith, poignant and evocative as that of the linkboy, who carried his flaming torch through the night-blanketed streets of eighteenth-century Liverpool, and from whom he claims proud lineage. And we—we shall be left with nothing but the memory of "Leerie" who has threaded his twinkling way through two centuries of Liverpool history.

WONDERS AND HORRORS IN LIME STREET

" The Chamber of Horrors used to be in this cellar," said my guide as he led me down a precarious flight of steps into the bowels of Lime Street.

Upstairs, the pipes and drums of a ceilidhe, which was in progress on the top floor, mingled their swirling music with the staccato clicking of balls on the billiard-tables which now occupy the other two floors of what was once Reynolds's famous Liverpool Waxworks.

" Of course everything has completely changed since old Reynolds's time," explained my companion in a voice which many years of life in Liverpool had not robbed of its granite-edged Scots accent, " the building has been practically gutted. Only the entrance hall and walls are as they used to be. As for the rest . . . you would think it had been stirred with a stick."

Looking around the bare, whitewashed basement it was difficult to realize that once upon a time thousands of people had paid their eager sixpences to feast upon the horrors which were the quondam tenantry of its arched recesses. Now, there was nothing more fearsome than the huge furnace crouched like a slumbering monster in the corner. Almost apologetically my guide said that it was rather dull nowadays, but his eyes lit up as he recalled that one day in 1922 he had stumbled upon a very fine cast of Charlie Peace's head, gruesomely divorced from any suggestion of a body, rolling in the rubble.

* * * *

It was round about the year 1860 that Alfred John Reynolds, the Tussaud of the provinces, decided to settle down in Liverpool. He came from his native Bristol via Birmingham, Leeds, Bradford and Manchester, and he brought his travelling waxworks with him. Looking about for a permanent home for his exhibition, his fancy lighted upon the old Freemasons' Hall in Lime Street. Here, he first established a dining-room and then, a year or two later, installed his effigies for what was to prove a stay of sixty years.

The new waxworks was a tremendous success from the start and perhaps its greatest attraction was that grisly section in the basement— why are such things always situated belowstairs ?—which Reynolds dubbed " The Criminal Chamber." Here were to be seen the waxen shades of most of the criminally illustrious of their day, and Charlie Peace was prime favourite in an unholy company which included such notables as Franz Müller the first railway murderer, Palmer the Rugeley poisoner, Mrs. Dyer the baby farmer and Mary Eleanour Pearcy the perambulator murderess.

The catalogue of the Criminal Chamber is an enchanting document written in the lost language of an age which combined relish for salty details with a tone of high moralising. Thus, of William Dove, executed at York in 1856 for the speeding of his spouse into happier realms with the aid of a liberal libation of strychnine, it says: "His parents were examples of kindness and humanity and gave their son a liberal education, having had him brought up at the College near Leeds ; but Nature, which baffles the calculations of man, formed him of a cruel disposition . . ."

Not far from Dove stood the stiff likeness of Captain Henry Rogers, " A jolly master (by repute), who systematically murdered members of his crew in the days when ships were sunk for the insurance money." This merry mariner was eventually hanged in grim old Kirkdale Gaol for the murder of Andrew Rose, a seaman aboard the *Martha and Jane.*

Reynolds always displayed a proper pride in this criminal gallery of his and spared neither effort nor expense to do the right thing by his public. Anxious to secure a model of James Berry, the master-hangman, he did not hesitate to pay that worthy craftsman the sum of £100 for sittings. During these sessions Mr. Hangman Berry whiled away the time with cosy little tales of the platform manners of various clients whom he had " turned off." At the time of Mrs. Maybrick's arrest in 1889, Reynolds was very keen to prepare a model of the accused in readiness to fill a place of honour should she be convicted. Unfortunately for him, before the trial began Mrs. Maybrick's mother—the Baroness de Roque—flitted frantically around buying up all the existing photographs of her daughter. Not to be thwarted, the single-minded Reynolds betook himself, sketch-book-in-hand, to the court and with the aid of drawings which he made of the woman in the dock constructed a very lifelike waxwork. Despite the subsequent offer of many hundreds of pounds from Mrs. Maybrick's affronted relatives, the wily old proprietor steadfastly refused to remove the offending effigy from his exhibition.

*　　*　　*　　*

Upstairs, where the shaded lamps made the tops of the billiard-tables look like so many smooth, green islands in the dusky sea of gloom which surrounded them, I stood in what had once been part of the Great Hall and my mind reached back to a February night practically seventy years ago. That night had been an historic one, for it had marked the 25th anniversary of the opening of his Liverpool

Waxworks, and Alfred Reynolds had celebrated with a grand banquet. At 11 p.m. precisely, some 300 guests had sat down at tables laid out in the centre of that vast hall of waxworks and there, watched by the glassy eyes of the silent dummies which crowded the shadows, they ate and drank beneath the brightly-flaring gas-lamps. An observer might be forgiven for thinking that sorcery was abroad that February evening, for, shifting his gaze from the still effigy of the Prince of Wales to the seat of honour at the main table, his astonished eyes would have discovered the Royal original occupying that place. The Master of Ceremonies called for silence and Mr. Reynolds rose and proposed the health of the Queen. Glasses were lifted and the Grand Orchestrion pealed forth the National Anthem. His Royal Highness responded for Her Majesty and the Grand Self-Acting Organ obliged with " God Bless the Prince of Wales." Prince von Bismarck raised his glass to " the prosperity of the institution," the chairman made graceful acknowledgement and the Beautiful Automaton Pianiste rendered a sparkling fantasia on one of Erard's Grand Pianofortes.

*   *   *   *

That glittering banquet represented the zenith of Reynolds's Waxworks. From then on it is a sad story of gradual decline. In 1913 the Waxworks hit the headlines again, but this time it was with a report of a social occasion of somewhat inferior calibre. Some burglars who had raided the adjoining warehouse of Messrs. Rylands had dropped into Reynolds's via a skylight and, having helped themselves to the contents of the refreshment bar, had descended to enjoy a picnic among their peers in the basement. Bottles of pop and cakes, with Crippen as guest of honour, were the highlight of their achievement.

During the years that followed various attempts were made to renew a waning public interest in the Gallery of Illustration by the importation of a number of freaks. There were the Orissa twins, Craio the missing link and the lion-headed boy : but the old Waxworks was dying, being strangled it was said by a new-fangled invention—animated pictures.

In the past the theatres had provided a certain competition but this had been successfully countered by the production of a series of pantomimes, *Blue Beard*, *Robinson Crusoe*, *Sinbad the Sailor* and the like, with marionettes as actors and actresses. Moving pictures, however, proved a more formidable foe. There was a final desperate flirtation with the enemy. A bioscope was installed and gave two shows daily. But it was all of no avail and in 1922 the auctioneer's hammer fell and finally shattered Reynolds's Waxworks.

Among the lots listed in the sale catalogue were some intriguing items—a model of Little Tich which danced and bowed ; an English execution with brand-new clockwork ; Ayella, a beautifully modelled female figure of a snake-charmer in handsome oriental dress with snakes and alligators and electric fittings for lighting up the snakes' eyes. There was also a bioscope and, representing perhaps the last concession to a conquering enemy, " Charlie Chaplin performing the splits with pretty movement of a bird in a tree."

PILLAR TO POST

P.B. No. 114 stands where the short dagger of Sefton Park Road thrusts at the sabre-curve of Croxteth Road. To the casual observer there is nothing to mark this very ordinary Edward VII period pillar-box as in any way different from any of the other 888 pillar-boxes which colourfully punctuate the grey pavements of the Liverpool Head Postmaster's area. But it is, in fact, a kind of ancient monument, standing as it does just a little to the east of the site of Liverpool's very first pillar-box. The story of this pioneer pillar-box goes back to the days of the Crimean War; to November 1854, to be precise. At that time, when British postal reformer, Sir Roland Hill, was still trying to persuade the Commissioners of Paving in London to approve pillar-boxes for the metropolis, the enterprising Liverpool postmaster gave an order to a local firm of iron-founders for a hollow cast-iron pillar, having a letter-slit on one side, and with a small door on the other, through which a letter-box could be inserted and removed. So it came about that, months before London saw its first pillar-box, the people of Liverpool's Sefton Park district were making regular use of one.

Just over a century ago, the pillar-box was only a traveller's tale in Britain. On the Continent, street mail-boxes had long been established. They probably derived from the invention of that nameless official of sixteenth-century Italy who fitted-up closed boxes, known as *Tamburi*, outside the churches of the Florentine Republic wherein could be placed, in safe anonymity, denunciations of State enemies.

In England, however, letters had to be taken to official receiving-houses for despatch. These places were far from numerous, and closed at an early hour in the afternoon. Urgent or late correspondence had to be handed to the bellman, a picturesque figure in a top-hat, scarlet swallow-tail coat and blue trousers, who had originally been employed by an eighteenth-century worthy, Charles Povey, who once ran his own halfpenny postal service. The bellman was really a kind of perambulating pillar-box. He used to parade the streets, ringing a handbell and carrying a locked bag provided with a slit for inserting letters, which, for a fee of one penny each, he would deliver to the central office. The bellman disappeared from the scene in 1846 when the receiving-houses were ordered to remain open until 7 p.m.

It was as part of his plans for the reform of British postal services that Roland Hill had, by 1840, suggested the adoption of pillar letter-boxes similar to those which he had seen in France. He managed to obtain approval for one to be installed in Westminster Hall, but the official side was not at all happy at the idea of " allowing precious missives to be committed to the interior of an unprotected box situated on the public footpath."

In 1851, in response to a request by the people of St. Helier, Jersey, for the number of town receiving-houses to be increased, an assistant post-office surveyor was sent to the Channel Islands. That surveyor was none other than Anthony Trollope, of Barsetshire fame, and it was as a result of his recommendations that, on November 23rd, 1852, the first roadside letter-boxes in Great Britain were erected—four on Jersey and three on Guernsey. These first boxes were four feet in height, they were of cast-iron, red in colour, and stood on a granite pedestal. Originally, they were hexagonal in shape, but they were later made octagonal by the insertion of two extra panels. They were an unqualified success from the start, and in March 1854, experimental pillar-boxes were erected at Cheltenham. By the September of that year, officialdom was at long last satisfied as to the suitability of the new amenities, and in 1855 London received its first six pillar-boxes. In the following year fifty new boxes were ordered, eleven of which went to Edinburgh, where they were hailed with such enthusiasm that before the interior fittings were complete they were filled to overflowing with mail !

Contrary to general expectation, early pillar-boxes were not abused, although street-urchins displayed a tendency to try and fill them up with sticks and stones, and from the first, November 5th brought its crop of pillar-box fires ! Nevertheless, they have sometimes been found to contain other things than letters. Pickpockets have been known to place wallets and purses in them after they have extracted the money, and in rural districts postmen have found birds nesting in them. A colony of snails once took up residence in one and used the letters for food. An unsolved mystery was the discovery of a cat and her kittens snugly ensconced among the letters !

During the twenty years following the installation of the first pillar-boxes, many different types were used. London's earliest half-dozen had proved unsatisfactory. They were all square, squat, heavy, iron contraptions, painted green and crowned with a fretted dome and an iron ball. Each bore a plate showing the distance to the General Post-Office and, on the sides, the legend " Post-Office Letter-Box." Their appearance was not good and they were too low. The indicator plates were constantly splashed with mud, and, even when clean, it was necessary to kneel on the pavement in order to read them.

The public poured in designs for new pillar-boxes, ranging from clock-towers to sign-posts. In 1856, hexagonal boxes, crusted with those brass ornamentations dear to the Victorian heart, and embellished with a compass-plate on the top, enjoyed a brief vogue. In the early days, blue, brown, green, bronze and yellow-painted boxes were employed indiscriminately, though green ones predominated. But in 1874, red was adopted as the standard colour, and now a special weather-resistant red paint, prepared from a carefully preserved formula, coats every pillar-box. Blue-painted boxes for the reception of air-mail letters joined the familiar red ones in 1930, but by 1938 the bulk of foreign mail was going by air, and the special boxes were withdrawn. In war time, pillar-boxes suddenly acquired bright yellow hats. This was due, however, to the fact that they were painted with a substance which reacted to the presence of gas, and was not for decorative purposes.

The year 1876 saw the introduction of the plain cylindrical box which has come to be the standard type mainly because it is more economical to maintain. Modern pillar-boxes are made in four styles. Three of these are cylindrical, single-aperture boxes, weighing $7\frac{1}{2}$ cwt., and one is an oval, double-fronted type, which weighs 19 cwt. There are also some eleven kinds of lamp and wall-boxes. Today, there are about 90,000 pillar, wall and lamp-boxes in the United Kingdom. That is approximately one to every 450 yards in urban districts, and one to every half-mile in populated country areas. Pillar-boxes are preferred, except where traffic is too small to warrant their erection, as they hold 800 letters, as compared with a mere 400 which is the maximum capacity of a wall-box.

The ordinary pillar-box is made of cast-iron. It is constructed in three sections, the cap, the door and the pillar, which are bolted together. The strong locks which are fitted to the doors have been made for over sixty years by one well-known firm, and the time-of-collection plates have also been made by one firm for nearly forty years. It was in Liverpool that the movable tablets which show the time of the next collection were first used. Invented by Mr. J. D. Rich, appointed Liverpool Postmaster in 1875, the device was intended not only for the convenience of the public, but also as a check on the activities of the postman. It is interesting to note that pillar-boxes, which are said to be immovable, are planted only eighteen inches in the ground, but they are bedded in concrete.

Although the average life of a pillar-box is assessed as being in the region of forty years, many Liverpool ones are of much greater age. Round about 1862 it was noticed that some pillar-boxes bore no evidence of being post-office property, so an experimental design, bearing a large crown on top, was manufactured, and six of these were erected in Liverpool. One was placed outside St. George's Hall in 1863. It was later moved to the front of Lime Street Post-Office, where it continued in use until 1938. A second, stood formerly in Exchange Flags, whence it was removed in 1938 when alterations were being made. It is now in the Post-Office Museum in London. Three crowned pillar-boxes still remain, however. One stands in Sheil Road, near the entrance to Newsham Park; one is situated at the junction of Breck and Everton Roads, and the third occupies the corner of St. Anne Street and Queen Anne Street. They are, all three, museum-pieces, strangely antiquated-looking in their present-day settings of busy streets, where, throughout six reigns, they have stood guard over countless sackfuls of Royal Mail.

PUBS WITH PERSONALITY

I drank my pint to the tapping of hammers and sadly reflected that it would not be long now before the old " Pig and Whistle " had finally vanished. Of course there will still be a tavern of that name in Covent Garden, but it will be a very different place from the quaint little pub which has existed in Liverpool for longer than anyone seems able to remember.

Even as I swallowed my beer, the unsentimental architects were busy prodding disapprovingly at age-eaten wood, shaking their heads and making significant entries in little black notebooks. All this was being done in the name of progress, and I supposed that the larger, more luxurious and up-to-date puolic-house which would result would be a technical improvement, but I know that I am not the only one who mourns the passing of yet another of the slender links which bind Liverpool to its past.

I sat in the tiny front parlour that day with landlord Reggie Brew. It was the very room in which the old ships' masters used to meet. You could still see there the curious rack for their tall hats and a high wooden pipe-rack in which the skippers would put their long church-wardens, confident that when they came back at the end of a voyage they would find them waiting there just as they had left them. All of that little room has now been swept away.

Outside in the hall, was a small bar, fronted by a very ancient-looking wire window, quite unlike anything else anywhere in Liverpool. That is going too. " I like it and am sad to see it done away with," said Mr. Brew, " but it really is hopelessly inconvenient." He brightened up, however, as he pointed to the unique brass plate which is fixed to the wall by the side of the door. " EMIGRANTS SUPPLIED " it says, and that simple statement, polished by legions of dead hands to the furthest fringe of legibility, conjures up fascinating pictures from the past. " We are preserving that," he added happily.

Leaving the " Pig and Whistle," my quest for a really old-world pub took me to Fenwick Street, where, behind a prim façade, hides the strangest of all Liverpool's taverns—the Slaughterhouse.

It was during the reign of George III that the wine-merchant, George Bennett, established his business in these ancient premises, and for nearly two centuries now, Liverpool gentlemen have delighted to sip their wine in this place which seems untouched by time.

You enter through an ordinary-looking wooden door upon which the word " WAREHOUSE " is still painted, and find yourself in a large room, crowded with huge sherry-butts, each as big as a man. All the drink here—spirits and beer alike—is drawn from the wood, and as you sit on the empty champagne cases which serve as seats savouring it, you soon discover that it has its own special flavour.

Everything about the Slaughterhouse whispers of the past. If you look up at the great black beams which traverse the ceiling you will see the hooks upon which, two hundred years ago, they used to hang the beasts.   For this really *was* a slaughterhouse once upon a time.

Then there is the Pillar of Coins upon which are nailed up all the pieces of counterfeit money that have been passed within these walls since the head of the third Hanoverian graced the coin of the realm.

Perhaps one of the most intriguing features of this tavern is the Rat Pit—a cosy little sanctum, beloved of the regulars, where, in the war years, hundreds of pounds were collected for the Red Cross.

In one corner of the main room there is a high, wire-fronted desk which stands on a dais. It is very old and the wood of its polished surface has been worn into runnels where countless coins have been scooped off it. It looks like one of those counting-house desks which one sees in woodcuts illustrating early editions of Dickens's novels.

Behind the desk presides Arthur, who, with his beaming pink face, pince-nez and shiny black alpaca jacket, resembles a Dickens character himself. Arthur has been forty-five years at the Slaughterhouse and says that he has seen few changes in that time. " Though," he added wryly, " the present generation don't consume anything like as much as their fathers did. In the old days men would drink a bottle of whisky without turning a hair." He remembers when the dealers used to trot horses up and down Fenwick Street and recalls the transactions which took place between the farmers and brokers. " I reckon more business was done in here than ever was in the Corn Exchange," he laughed. " They would bring in samples of corn, barley, maize and the like : you were walking on it all the time."

I doubt if anyone would contest the Slaughterhouse's claim to be the oldest licensed house in Liverpool, but if they did the challenge would almost certainly come from Dale Street.

Dale Street was once Liverpool's street of taverns and boasted the majority of the town's coaching-inns.   Today, only a couple of that great company remain. " The Angel " survives on the corner of North John Street, but it is now a hotch-potch of shops and offices, the merest corner of which carries on its old tradition of supplying the wants of travellers' dusty throats.

Almost opposite it, " The George," founded in 1726, still flourishes. It has been rechristened " Rigby's." Here is a panelled back-room which, with its low-beamed ceiling and ships' lanterns, manages to suggest the chartroom of one of those old-time wooden men-of-war. A brass ship's clock of recent date strikes the one anachronistic note. Close beside this clock hangs a fine oil-painting of Nelson's ship *Victory*, together with a framed reproduction of the neat rows of coloured flags which spelt out the historic Trafalgar signal " England expects every man will do his duty." From an adjoining wall gaze the austere features of Nelson himself, whilst over the mantelpiece is exhibited the *pièce de résistance* of this veritable Nelson Museum. It is nothing less than a contract partly written in the great admiral's own manuscript. Addressed to Messrs. John and William Woodhouse, merchants of Marsala at Palermo, it is dated March 19th, 1800, and is an agreement between them and the right Honourable Rear-Admiral Horatio Lord Nelson, K.B., Duke of Bronte in Sicily, to furnish His Majesty's ships off Malta with five hundred pipes of the best Marsala wine. When Nelson received this consignment, he is alleged to have been asked to give the wine a name. " Call it Bronte," said His Lordship. " But Bronte means thunder," protested his minions. " It will do very well," insisted Nelson, " John Bull will not know what it means and will think all the better of it on that account."

Just round the corner in Hackins Hey is " Ye Hole in Ye Wall," which, if we are to believe the date which appears over the magnificent, brass-canopied fireplace, was also founded in the year 1726.

A curious feature of this house is that the cellar is situated upstairs and beer, drawn from a tap and not a pump, is served to you in special glasses decorated with an engraving of a fragment of brick wall.

I had intended to go on to inspect several other pubs with personality. I wanted to visit " The Muck Midden," " Ma Egerton's " and " Ye Cracke " in Rice Street, where, to this day, may be seen a little snug which bears the legend " THE WAR OFFICE " upon its glass fanlight. The name is an echo from the troubled days when old men used to forgather in that cubby-hole to discuss the progress of the Boer War. So persistently did those bar-parlour militarists discourse upon the niceties of tactics, so vehemently did they lay down the laws of strategy and ferociously debate the conduct of the war, that some wag decided to bestow upon the old campaigners the fragile immortality of that unique glass memorial.

I had intended, I say, to see all these places.

Alas, for the frailty of human nature : I seem to have got stuck in " Ye Hole in Ye Wall " ! The truth of the matter is that, overcome by the prodigious hospitality of a series of mine hosts, I foolishly fell into conversation with a stout and happy-looking man by the bar who kept insisting on filling my glass with whisky. Moreover, he embroiled me in some fearful calculation which, for no reason that I could discover, involved the multiplication of MDCCXXVI (the inscription over the aforesaid fireplace) by CC—the whole process to be conducted in Roman numerals. It was all too much for me. Feebly, I gave up the ghost and concentrated on the spirits.

STREET OF WATER

Behind the drab no-man's-land of Pall Mall, contrasting strangely with the busy, bustling Mersey, stretches Liverpool's forgotten waterway—the Leeds and Liverpool Canal.

Three-quarters of the way down Pall Mall there stands a crumbling, red brick building above the door of which is still to be seen the legend "LEEDS & LIVERPOOL CANAL COMPANY." But the building has been blitzed: the company is no more: the doorway to the canal is barred. And when I went there the other day, it was only through the kindness of William Leech that I was able to see the canal-basin at all.

Mr. Leech is one of the directors of a firm of tarpaulin manufacturers and the back of his workshop abuts upon the source of the canal. He led me through a large shed where men, seated at outsize sewing-machines, stitched busily away at the stiff canvases. "We used to make hundreds of tarpaulins for the barges but now they are mainly for lorries," said Mr. Leech. Then, suddenly, he opened a little door and there was the canal lapping his doorstep.

At first, the flat, wide expanse of water looked like a dull, dark sheet of glass, and then the sun came out and sent a thousand reflected ripples darting and shimmering on the smoke-black surfaces of old stone walls. But even in the sunlight, it is a haunted waterway, along which glide lonely, ghost-like barges which bring coal to Liverpool and carry sugar, wool and grain to the wild dales of Yorkshire. There is about it a tranquil, brooding air which belongs to the past. That is scarcely to be wondered at when you remember that its foundation dates back to 1774, just thirteen years after Francis Egerton, the jilted Duke of Bridgewater, drove England's first commercial canalway between Manchester and his estate at Worsley. During practically two centuries, the Leeds and Liverpool Canal has seen many changes in the landscape of its banks. The prosperous residential quarter which once surrounded it has disappeared, and today it meanders through a huddled decay of dark warehouses and satanic mills which are the legacy of that industrial revolution which it itself made possible.

"It is absolutely dead," the voice of Mr. Leech cut into my reverie, "they should fill it in. I remember the time when you would see forty or fifty boats in a week. Now . . ." with a wave of his

45

hand he indicated the derelict barges, black skeletons slowly disintegrating at their moorings. He pointed to some nearby warehouses. " Those used to be loading basins but there was no use for them so they filled them in and built storage sheds in their place." As we picked our way carefully between the huge sheets of outstretched tarpaulin which covered practically all the floor, Mr. Leech told me that once upon a time this part of his factory had been the premises of the Boatman's Mission, where the Reverend Mr. Henrikssen, a Norwegian clergyman, had established a small club in which the bargees could enjoy tea and cakes and a good game of billiards.

Having seen the hidden basin of the canal, I went through an iron gate and down a patchy grass ramp to the towpath. In view of the fact that Mr. Leech had said that it was unlikely that I would find any barges on the canal that afternoon, I was both surprised and delighted when the *Richard* hove into sight. Slowly, she chugged up to where I was standing and then . . . passed right by and disappeared. A workman, seeing the dismay in my face, hastily explained, " He's only going to whan her." To " whan " is bargees' language and means to turn the barge round.

Mr. G. W. Grundy, the skipper of the *Richard*, was a real discovery. Rising seventy, although to look at his red, weather-beaten face you would never guess it, he has been on barges ever since he was nine years old. His parents were both water-folk, he proudly told me, and his mother is still alive and hearty at ninety-one, after a lifetime up and down the canals of England. She lives on land now, in a little house in Wigan. " There aren't any family boats on the Leeds and Liverpool nowadays," said Mr. Grundy, " though you'll find them on the Shropshire Union." The skipper invited me aboard his barge, a resplendent affair, painted with those brilliant colours which one sees at fairgrounds. I followed him down a short ladder into a small cabin. It was only about four feet high and there was not room for a man to stand erect. It was furnished sparsely ; wooden forms to sit on, a folding wooden table and a miniature stove. We had a cup of tea together down there, a hurried one, as the skipper had not much time to spare. He was going back to Wigan—by train !

As I watched Mr. Grundy's figure fade into the distance, his clogs clattering along the stone parapet, I decided to pay a visit to the lock-keeper's cottage a short way up the canal. There, I found Mr. Robert Vincent Ball, an ex-navy man who has water in his blood and loves his job. " I have been at this lock since February 1941," he told me, " and I was here right through the blitz by myself." Mr. Ball lives all alone in his cottage by the water's edge: alone, that is, except for " Princess "—" Only a mongrel but she's real faithful "—and " Minnie," the tabby-kitten which he found swimming desperately for her life in the canal. He cooks, sews and does his own housework. In a glass-fronted room, rather like the bridge-house of a ship, he showed me the book in which he has to enter the name and details of every craft which comes up from the Mersey, via Stanley Basin and the long flight of four locks in his charge, to the canal. The journey can be accomplished in the remarkably short space of twenty-five minutes. Mr. Ball emptied one of the locks for my benefit. I timed the operation. The water dropped fifteen feet in seven minutes.

It was growing dusk when at last I retraced my steps to the canal-basin. I came up from the bank on to a little iron bridge and there I found the Bridge Inn which might be fairly described as the Liverpool headquarters of the bargees. Here, in his cosy public, landlord John Murphy introduced me to some of the really wonderful characters who bring a rich vein of colour to the leaden waterways. There they sat in the coarse blue jerseys, bright neckerchiefs and clogs which are the unofficial uniform of the men who navigate the inland waterways. I was very lucky that evening because Uncle Joe happened to be there. Uncle Joe is famous along the length and breadth of every canal in the north of England. His real name is Tom Cheetham and with him were four other Toms—Tom Abrahams, Tom Baybudd, Tom Bowen, and his bosom friend, Tom Marsden.

I had a long chat with Tom Baybudd. Tom is another of those fast vanishing men who have spent all their lives on the canal. " It's a hard life but I have no regrets except one : I never learned to read or write." The eldest boy in a family of twelve, he was kept much too busy to attend school. " It's not nice," he said sadly, the soft burr that betrayed Burscough lending a queer attractiveness to his voice, " it's not nice. You see other chaps reading the paper and you can't. I even have to get people to read my letters for me. These days there are special schools at various points along the canals and when the boats tie-up the barge children have to attend them." All at once the humour drained from his face : his eyes became very serious. " Every lad and lass has a right to scholarship," he said quietly, " and I want to see ALL of them taught to read and write, to have a chance that my generation never had." And then, in a minute, he was laughing and joking again.

Certainly, they were a merry crowd, those bargees, but when at length the talk turned to the present state of the canals, a note of sadness crept into their voices. They all remembered the good old days of the horse-drawn barges when canals were still important transport lines in the economic life of the country, and mourned their passing. Uncle Joe, gazing reflectively into the amber depths of his beer-glass, began to recall remote canal-side inns, which, like the posting-houses of the coaching era, were once recognised stages, where generation upon generation of bargees would tie-up their boats, stable their horses and forgather in the snug to gossip and yarn over a pint just as we were doing at the Bridge Inn that evening. But that is all past and today the majority of those snugs are empty of water-folk and an unwonted silence of neglect hovers above the unruffled, evening surfaces of the many deserted water-lanes of England which flow forlornly by their doors.

PUTTING A BRAVE FACE ON IT

SOMEHOW I can't shake off the feeling that if anyone were to ask me the name of my club and I had to reply " The Ugly Face Club," even the blandishments of those friends who would compliment me upon the nicety of my choice, and the sympathy of those enemies who regretted it, would not propitiate a certain embarrassment which the admission would cause me.

And yet, strange to relate, there did once exist in this city of surprises a club which rejoiced in just that title, and I have before me as I write a copy of the membership register upon which are inscribed the names of 55 brave Liverpool gentlemen who unhesitatingly acknowledged their physical qualifications for entry upon the roll of such a society.

⋆ ⋆ ⋆ ⋆

Ye Ugly Face Clubb of Leverpoole, or to give it its full and proper style, ' Ye Most Honourable and Facetious Society of Ugly Faces,' was formed on January 15th, 1743, and seems to have continued in existence for eleven years, until January 21st, 1754.

Its members appear to have been drawn chiefly from the merchant class—the ugly faces of commerce !—though one distorted doctor of divinity, three or four mean-visaged medicos, several squint-eyed ships' captains and a sprinkling of toad-faced tradesmen were included in its ill-formed body.

The primary condition for membership was that the aspiring candidate should exhibit " something odd, remarkable, Drol or out of the way in his Phiz, as in the length, breadth, narrowness, or in his complexion, the cast of his eyes, or make of his mouth, lips, chin, &c." The fortunate possessor of such features as a deathbed complexion, a hedgehog forehead, squinting, pig eyes, a " monstrous long nose resembling a speaking trumpet " or one " rising in the

49

middle like a camel's hunch," a fluke mouth with " irregular bad set teeth like those of an old worn-out comb thoroughly begrim'd " and a tongue like an anchovy, or a " prodigeous long chin meeting his nose like a pair of nutcrackers," was always sure of sympathetic consideration. His suitability for membership was judged of by the majority of the Society, the President having the casting vote.

★   ★   ★   ★

How well some of the members merited election is apparent from the descriptions of them which have been left for the envy of posterity.

Captain Nicholas Southworth. A fine yellow guinea complexion. Large nostrils. Negro nosed. Hollow forehead. Long pucking chin. In ye whole resembles Tom Thumb in a puppet show.

Robert Moss, Esq., Councellor at Law. A long tawny visage. Lanthorn jawed. Hollow pig eyes. Large nose. A prodigious wide mouth, especially when he laughs, and looks like a Grubb Street Poett half starv'd.

Mr. Jno. Wood. July 22, 1751, of Liverpool, Architect. A stone coloured complexion. A dimple in his attic storey. The pillasters of his face fluted. Tortoise eyed. A prominent nose, wild grin and face altogether resembling a badger, and finer though smaller than Sir Christopher Wren or Inigo Jones's.

Thos. Wycliffe, Merchant in Liverpool, 22 Jany., 1753. A ghostlike complexion. Goggle eyed. A fine shrivelled face. A marl pit in his chin. Furrows in his cheeks. Bushy eyebrows. On the whole picture of a hard winter with a ghastly grin.

Henry Spendilow. A rugged face. A large, flattish nose. A fluke mouth. Thick lips. Lank jaws. Long chin. In short a charming member in every respect.

James Ashton, D.D., Chaplain to ye Society. A fine carved face. Eyelashes like two besoms. Nose like a shuffle nosed shark. Blubber lips. Meagre cheeks. A triangular mouth. Eyes of a sea green. Exceedingly well qualified member.

The President, Jos. Farmer, merchant, was, as befitted his office, unbelievably hideous—" Little Eyes one bigger than y' other. Long Nose. Thin Lanthorn Jaws. Bare upper Lip. Mouth from Ear to Ear resembling a shark's. Rotten Sett of Irregular Teeth wch are sett off to great Advantage by frequent laughing. His Visage long and narrow. His looks upon the whole extraordinary, Haggard, Odd, Comick, and out of y' way. In short, possessed of every Extraordinary Qualifications to rend him y' Phoenix of y' Society, as the Like won't appear again this 1000 years."

Far from being offended by this frank assessment of his personal charms, Mr. Farmer, on being asked to accept office, wrote :

"I return you my *Hearty Thanks* for being Chosen *President* of yᵉ Most Ancient, Numerous and Honourable Fraternity of Ugly-Faces ; to wᶜʰ have belonged the greatest Heroes, Statesmen, Poets, Saints and Philosophers ; as Homer, Alexander, Æsop, Socrates, St. Paul, Cromwell, etc., who were all as eminently remarkable for their Ugly Grotesk Phizzes as for their several Great Abilities and Extensive Knowledge."

★　★　★　★

Our information concerning the Club's proceedings is unfortunately very scant. Indeed, had it not been for the wind of chance which, sometime in the late 'eighties of the last century, blew a curious old manuscript volume into the hands of Mr. Edward Howell, a Liverpool bookseller, it is doubtful if we should ever have heard of the Club at all.

The motto of the Society was "*Taetrum ante omnia vultum*," which may be rendered, "Before all things, an ugly face," and the members met once a fortnight at the Exchange Coffee House and dined together every three months.

The rules stipulated that every person upon his being initiated into the Society should drink a bumper to the success thereof, and that "ale shall be the common drink."

The income of the Society was mainly derived from 'forfeitures' or fines, and occasional collections. Expenditure was not high, on average somewhere about £15 a year, and that was chiefly spent on eating and drinking. There are, however, one or two intriguing items such as, "By paid the barber a year's attendance, 6s.," "To cash paid the servant for Dressing a Pigg" (not a member this, one trusts !), and, most fascinating of all, "By Miss Betty Wrigley a tickett, 2s."

The members were, not surprisingly, all bachelors, and Rule Number 11 laid down "That when any member Marries he shall forfeit ten shillings and sixpence for the use of this Society." That a number of such half-guineas were in the course of time duly received only goes to show that then, as now, love was blind, beauty only skin deep and residing in the eye of the beholder.

HAUNTED MERSEYSIDE

Being an Agony in Four Fits

Fit the First

GHOSTS OVER MERSEYSIDE

Faces that peer at you through a mist.
Cold hands that stroke your throat and pluck at your bedclothes.
Eerie footsteps that ring out in the still watches of the night.
The shadow form, half glimpsed, that glides through a winter dusk.

Ghosts !

" You may be an undigested bit of beef," apostrophised Scrooge, " a blot of mustard, a crumb of cheese, a fragment of underdone potato," but for all that Jacob Marley's ghost continued to confront him clanking his chains and wringing his shadowy hands.

There are many people who, like the old miser in Dickens's Christmas story, will glibly tell you that " There's more of gravy than of grave " about those apparitions which we call ghosts, an assertion which it is difficult to deny. By their very nature, ghosts are impossible entities to assess. You can't put them in test-tubes or under the microscope ; dissection and material analysis are out of the question, and objective investigation is all too frequently hampered by clouds of witnesses. Nevertheless, the belief in ghosts is as old as man himself, and from the earliest times there have been uneasy whisperings of unbidden guests who have made the night hideous and of weird happenings and hauntings which, defying all attempts at natural explanation, have struck terror into the hearts of those who have encountered them.

Among the masses of ghost stories which have troubled the centuries, many are patently ridiculous, many more are to be accounted for in terms of ignorance, superstition, indigestion, over-heated imagination and plain delusion. But there are others which are not so easily explained away, they are too well attested and rest upon firm foundations of evidence supplied by scientific and critically-minded observers.

52

Of recent years, the ghost has been at something of a discount: the whilom phantoms which were the beckoning ones outside the nursery window seem to have been ousted by Martians and space-visitors who stem from another kind of fantasy. It is the flying-saucer now and not the broom-bestriding witch that flashes past the moon's pale face! But there are still certain seasons of the year—Christmas for instance—that flee the mind to inglenooks and snug Pickwickian nights, when the old-fashioned spectre comes into its own, the magic carpet is unrolled and folk love to cluster in cosy horror round the spurting fire to tell tales of *things* that lurk in the shadows beyond the circle of its light.

It is in this mood of faintly sceptical nostalgia, that I have been turning back the pages of local history and going out into the streets and lanes to investigate the rich lore of ghosts over Merseyside.

One of the most singular cases which I have unearthed concerns a house situated in a central Liverpool district. It will, unfortunately, be necessary for me to refer to many of the scenes of ghostly disturbances in such vague terms, because a house which is reputed to be haunted is often difficult to let, so difficult in fact that no landlord will thank you for spreading the tale of its haunting abroad.

In the year 1934, a Mr. C. Collins, who at that time was the proprietor of a Brownlow Hill bookshop, had the misfortune to purchase the aforesaid apparently desirable residence in central Liverpool, and took with him to his new home a sizeable family consisting of his 78-year-old mother, his two grown-up daughters, a brother and sister and a couple of friends, Mr. Ben Griffiths and his sister, who were to lodge with the Collins's.

" We spent a good deal on the house in one way and another," lamented Mr. Collins later, " I wish we had saved ourselves the trouble now, for we could not live there any longer after what we have gone through." It was to Mr. Ben Griffiths that there came the first indication that the house was a troubled one. His was a room on the top floor, and on the very first night he spent in it his rest was disturbed by a continuous subdued whispering which seemed to come from a trap-door in the ceiling. A little later he was alarmed by the sound of footsteps as though someone was " walking stealthily to and fro wearing dancing-pumps." The phenomena went on for about a week and were always accompanied by a cold little wind which blew across his bed. Then one night *something* began to pull very gently at his bedclothes. That was really too much. Voices and footsteps were one thing, but an invisible hand plucking at your blankets . . . He made up his mind to tell Mr. Collins the whole story. To his surprise, Collins confessed that he too had heard footsteps and felt the cold breeze. They agreed not to tell any of the others of their uncanny experiences for fear of frightening them, but now the occurrences began to become more unnerving. One night the shadowy form of a young man stepped out from a wardrobe door, walked towards the window and vanished. He appeared to be about eighteen or nineteen years of age and, moving in a kind of grey mist, threw a queer half-shadow on the wall. Once, when Mr. Griffiths was lying in bed, a face suddenly materialised close to his own and peered at him through a cloud of vapour. A crucifix hung at the head of Griffiths's bed, and he afterwards attributed his safety to its presence, for he heard a voice say in his ear one evening, " Only one thing stops me from getting at you." Mr. Collins's mother also had an alarming experience when, one night, she felt a small hand like that of a child stroking her throat. The climax came when Mr. Collins's daughter, Lily, arrived home very late from a dance. Her father was woken by loud cries of " Come quickly," and found the girl in a swoon outside his bedroom door. Trembling, she told him how upon her return something had followed her up the dark stairway. Gaining her room, she had undressed quickly and jumped into bed. No sooner had she done so, than she heard footsteps in the room and when she called to her father they seemed to turn and come at her with a run. Then she felt a heavy weight as if someone had leapt on the bed. The family spent the remainder of the night downstairs huddled round the fire. The next day they left the house for good, and, said Mr. Collins, " Although I am a poor man, I wouldn't spend another night there for a hundred pounds."

By way of contrast with the foregoing authentic and apparently inexplicable—at any rate, unexplained—manifestations, I will now tell you of the farcical affair of the Ghost Pictures of Harrington Schools. It is a case which demonstrates very forcibly the power of mass hysteria and provides an object-lesson in just how careful one must be before assigning to any occurrence, no matter how many people may vouch for its genuineness, a supernatural origin.

The first muted suggestion that something was amiss at the school premises in Stanhope Street came at mid-day on Monday, June 7th, 1926, when a young boy returned home for lunch with a breathless tale of having seen the likeness of a human face imprinted on the glass of one of the school-room windows overlooking Grafton Street.

Throughout the long sultry hours of that far-away June afternoon, the story of the phantom face was passed from ear to credulous ear. Women neglected their household chores to gossip on their steps and when, with lengthening shadows, evening fell and the menfolk came home from work, the tale was told all over again, embellished now and ornate with all manner of details and artistic refinements which had at first been lacking.

By now a drizzle of rain had begun to fall, but, nothing deterred, hundreds of people started to flock eagerly to Stanhope Street. The drizzle became a downpour, but still the crowds came to stand doggedly there in the rain just staring at the school windows. Suddenly an excited woman gave a loud cry: " There . . . look . . . on that window, the figure of Christ carrying the cross ! " There was a buzz of excitement and men and women knelt down in the roadway and upon the rain-greased pavement.

As the evening wore on, the street became the scene of frenzied pilgrimage. Far into the night the people continued to come, a heterogenous collection of whites, negroes and Chinamen, who gazed reverently at what they were now calling the spirit pictures. A bluish smudge on one window was unhesitatingly identified as a thorn-crowned head and another became the Good Shepherd gathering His flock. An elderly woman who was still watching at midnight swore that a star appeared flickering in the centre of one of the panes of glass and that the colours of the pictures became as plain and clear as if it had been broad daylight.

In the small hours, a hastily summoned official of the school went round whitewashing a great many of the windows, but nevertheless when next morning the crowds gathered again it was not long before they had discovered upon another window a mirage effect which glistened in the sunshine and which was confidently hailed as the figure of the Virgin Mary standing in a rainbow.

By mid-morning, the congestion in the street had grown to such proportions as to have become something of a problem and the police were obliged to take a hand. Thereafter, each person was allowed a single glance and was then asked to " Move along, please."

Naturally, the pupils at the school became wildly excited when they saw the huge congregation in the roadway and lessons that day were carried on with considerable difficulty. Nor was it only the children's routine which suffered. The headmaster was besieged by a number of spiritualists and devout members of the public and, as he after-wards confessed, so impressed was he by the wonder and awe of the crowds that at one stage he had been loth to touch the windows, fearing that any such action on his part might be very fiercely resented.

Of course the headmaster himself was under no delusion as to the real nature of the marks on the windows which were the innocent cause of all the trouble. He said that when he had first come to the school he had noticed certain curious flaws in the window-panes. On investigation he found that the explanation was that the glass for many of these windows had been bought cheaply and had been previously used in shop-windows where it had been crusted with advertisements. The school window-cleaner confirmed that it was still possible to trace old lettering, vague eulogies of various brands of soap and chocolate, and said that in one sheet you could clearly see the imprint of a man's hand.

During the week immediately previous to that which saw the outbreak of the furore, the windows had been cleaned with paraffin, and it was the streaks of paraffin, together with the markings which were actually in the substance of the glass itself, which had been responsible for all the alleged phenomena.

In the course of the next night the remaining windows were duly treated with whitewash and the ghost pictures of Harrington Schools vanished like so many spectres at cock-crow. Indeed, you might say that the whole thing fizzled out like a damp squib in a window-cleaner's bucket.

But do not feel too comfortably secure in the belief that all such occurrences end with satisfactory material explanations, for I will tell next of some Liverpool hauntings for which reason can supply no such adequate answer.

HAUNTED LIVERPOOL

In many unexpected parts of present-day Liverpool you will chance upon remote streets of fine old houses behind whose massive walls, which once formed the bastions beyond which were cradled the secure lives of merchant princes and other men of substance, there now live perhaps a dozen families who, like the houses that shelter them, have fallen victim to the economic rigours of this day and age. Such places resemble nothing so much as seedy museums, and that, in a way, is just what they are, for embalmed within the walls of the houses which form them are such memories as ghosts—if ghosts there be—must thrive on.

I know of one such house in which there is a room where a family of four have their being. It is a drab, gloomy apartment and its history is known to me. In that room a retired major, who doted too much upon the bottle, lived nightmare hours filled with those hideous things which emerge from too many empty bottles, and, shortly after the turn of the century, slit his throat from ear to ear. Is it too much to think that this incident, and others like it, may well have charged the atmosphere with something of the electric horror which accompanied its perpetration, or that unwholesome things might be attracted to sites where such frightful dramas have been enacted? Indeed, such theories seem tacitly confirmed by the fact that many hauntings, particularly historic ones, centre upon localities which are the scenes of past violence and brutality. Similarly, it has been postulated by those who devote their lives to the investigation of psychic phenomena, that the spirits of those who have " passed over " will sometimes return to places which hold memories of old happiness for them. Such ghosts are harmless, vaguely whimsical entities, and have been said to have manifested themselves in many parts of the British Isles.

It is to this class of phantom, I feel sure, that two spectres who paid a visit some years ago to a house in one of Liverpool's declining squares, belonged. The people who owned the house had gone abroad, leaving strict instructions with the servants that on no account were any strangers to be admitted during their absence as there were many valuables in the house. One day, shortly after their departure, a carriage and pair drew up at the front porch, a footman assisted a lady and a little boy to alight, and, as the lady rang the bell, the carriage drove rapidly away. When the maid answered the door, the lady asked permission to look over the house. Remembering her employers' instructions, the maid replied that she was afraid that would not be possible, whereupon the little boy burst into tears and his companion began to entreat her to reconsider her verdict, urging that she had vital reasons for wishing to view the interior. At last the housemaid gave way. Once inside, the stranger seemed thoroughly at home, running up and down the stairs and moving confidently from room to room without enquiry or hesitation. At length, stepping into a dressing-room adjoining one of the main bedrooms, she suddenly raised both her hands and, exclaiming in tones of the deepest gratitude, " God bless you for what you have done for me this day," she and the boy both vanished into thin air. The terrified housemaid searched the place from cellar to attic, the police were called in and they too combed the house, but with the same result, the mysterious visitors had completely disappeared and were never seen again.

Some years later, a visitant of a rather different kind plagued the peace of an old house in Sackville Street, Everton. Whatever it was, this intruder was decidedly malignant and its activities led directly to a woman being detained in hospital. The mystery began shortly after the woman, together with her family and those of two of her relatives, moved into the house. On the first night of their tenancy a house-warming party was arranged, and it was at about nine o'clock in the evening, when the fun and games were at their height, that one of the guests became alarmed by the sound of eerie footsteps moving about somewhere in the attic reaches. A search was made but revealed nothing to account for the noises. Unnerved, however, some of the women insisted upon the police being called. Three men left the first-floor room where the festivities were being held, to make their way to the local police-station. Barely had they gone, when a terrific crash brought the women, screaming with fright, to the top of the stairs. Below, in a dazed state, lay one of the men. He had been descending the stairs, he said, preceded by one of his companions and followed by the other, when he felt two hands grasp him round the waist, lift him as though he were a mere toy and send him gliding down the stairway. " I seemed to be wafted down," are the words he actually used. During the next three nights the house was filled with strange noises and the occupants were too scared to sleep. Eventually, they reached a unanimous decision to quit the place, and agreed to move all the furniture down to the ground-floor. The three men went upstairs to start on the job. One of the ladies followed them up and was nearly at the top of the first flight when she gave a piercing shriek. Her terrified relatives, rushing out into the hall, watched in open-eyed horror as they saw the woman float a few feet in the air, stay poised there for a second or two, and then come gliding down to where they stood fourteen feet below. According to their testimony, the woman kept her arms outstretched throughout her flight, her eyes were wide and staring and she seemed to be surrounded by a kind of halo of light. She dropped on her feet with her arms still extended and then shot through a doorway into a room. When the others followed her they found her unconscious and she was later taken to hospital suffering from multiple injuries and nervous shock. Just who or what it was in that house in Sackville Street that delighted in hurling people down the stairs was never discovered, but then no one knows what strange or horrible thing may have happened, far-away and long-ago, within its bland brick walls.

With its bright lights and constant traffic of pleasure, the Lime Street area is probably one of the last places in which you might expect to encounter a ghost, and yet a Mr. and Mrs. Cuthbert Wilkinson met two in a private hotel within easy walking distance of Lime Street Station. During the first night he spent there, Mr. Wilkinson awoke with a start and the impression that the echo of some loud noise was still ringing in his ears. Suddenly wide awake, he sat up in bed and saw in the moonlight which poured a cold stream through a nearby window, the figure of a tall girl in a light-coloured frock, apparently intent upon searching the pockets of his overcoat which was hanging behind the door. Thinking that she was a thief, Mr. Wilkinson promptly threw one of his shoes at her and to his dismay it passed right through the girl's body. She turned her head in his direction but seemed to be staring at something behind him. Uneasily, he looked round to see what she was gazing at so intently, but saw nothing. When he looked back to where the woman had been she had vanished. Instantly, he leapt out of bed and ran to the door. It was locked on the inside. Shaking violently, maybe because it was a cold night, maybe chilled by what was a most frightening experience, he scrambled hurriedly back into bed and pulled the blankets over his head. Later on in the course of their stay, Mrs. Wilkinson, too, was vouchsafed a ghostly glimpse. She was in the bedroom one evening preparing to go out. Crossing to the wardrobe to get her raincoat, she heard someone give a little cough behind her. Turning round, she saw facing her a very tall man in a bright check suit. He had dark, piercing eyes, black hair and a moustache, and she noticed that he held one arm in a sling. For a second or two he stood gazing straight into her face, then he walked to the window, which was wide open at the bottom, and leaned out. Recovering from her surprise, Mrs. Wilkinson ran from the room, but remained standing on the landing within full view of the door so that no one could leave by it without her seeing them, while a maid went for help. When the maid returned with the manager's wife and the hall-porter, they made a thorough search of Mrs. Wilkinson's room but found no trace of the mysterious intruder. The hotel in question has since been converted into offices.

Another one-time hotel—or rather lodging-house—situated in the heart of Liverpool's Sailor Town, and now converted into a garage, has boasted a ghost for at least sixty years. The phenomena follow a more or less standard pattern of footsteps, doors which will not remain closed and so forth. On several occasions the figure of a man dressed in the clothes of an old-time sailor has been seen, always in the same front room and always by the fireside. Again, one is not surprised by the advent of an apparition in such a locale for many of the old Liverpool seamen's lodging-houses were most vicious places from which the shellback was lucky to escape with his life, let alone his money-belt.

Next, the black limelight switches to the spectres of suburbia, and I will recount how I spent a windswept night keeping a tryst with a phantom in plum-coloured trousers upon a desolate beach at Garston.

SPECTRES IN SUBURBIA

It was a wild churchyard night with the moon chasing the shadows, and anyone seeing our two figures upon the beach would have been hard put to explain why a couple of apparently sane men should be pacing the river-front at twelve o'clock on such a night. Had they questioned us and been told " We are here to keep a date with a ghost," they would most probably have revised their opinions concerning our sanity and have taken to their heels.

But there was no one there.

A savage wind tore at the clattering corrugated-iron fence of the bottle factory and drove stinging drops of rain into our faces. Over to the left stretched a barren dyke-rutted waste land, across which the flashing blue airfield location beacon of Speke Airport cast the periodic brilliance of its raking beam. In front of us, the murky-looking river and, looming stark and skeletal in the darkness, the battered hulk of a beached ship.

We had come to this forlorn fragment of foreshore because of a most unpleasant experience which had befallen my companion, Mr. William Routledge, who has a ship-breaking yard at this spot, one November night in 1951. At that time Mr. Routledge was engaged in breaking up a hundred-year-old, three-masted, German barque called the *Fides*, and, anxious to fetch the vessel further in at high-water, which was due at 1 a.m., Routledge, his wife and his sister-in-law had piled into his car and driven down to the Garston waterfront at the bottom of Brunswick Street.

In view of what I am about to relate, I think it is only fair to tell you something about Bill Routledge himself. He is a big, greying man, an open-air type, who has done a lot of boxing in his youth and strikes you as a bluff, hearty sort of fellow with a strictly no-stuff-and-nonsense attitude to life. He is not by any means given to seeing visions and has been a lifelong teetotaller.

When, on that dark November night, Routledge and the two women reached the river end of the yard, they got out of the car and stood for some time looking at the *Fides* which was illuminated by the bright beams of the headlights. It was while they were standing thus, that Routledge's sister-in-law became aware of a slight movement on the waste ground on their left. She drew his attention to it, but, thinking that they had perhaps surprised a courting couple, Routledge tactfully told her to ignore it. A moment later, however, she was tugging at his sleeve again and, following her gaze, he saw an immense figure of a man rise out of the waste land. The man seemed to be of huge stature: "He looked at least six foot six," Mr. Routledge told me, " and I was particularly struck by his hair which stood up from his head in a great bush four or five inches high." There was something about the creature's demeanour which Routledge found vaguely uncanny. At that moment, the thing began to advance towards them. Its gait was curiously stooped like that of a great ape. On and on it came, walking right across the yawning black gap of a dyke as if it were treading solid ground instead of the empty air. Then, as they watched, the figure passed right through the headlights of the car without breaking their beam, and disappeared before the corrugated-iron fence. Both Routledge and his sister-in-law saw the apparition, and noticed that his clothes were curiously old-fashioned, his breeches in particular impressed them as peculiar, for they were tight, tapering and plum-coloured. One of the most extraordinary, and in my opinion significant, features of the whole affair was the fact that while Routledge and his wife's sister saw exactly the same thing, Mrs. Routledge, who stood beside them throughout the manifestation, saw nothing at all.

On the night of our vigil conditions were, as I have indicated, certainly all that any self-respecting spectre could desire. We waited there for fully two hours, smoking our pipes and stamping our feet, as the keen wind cut through heavy coats which felt as if they were made of tissue-paper. But there was never a sign of the ghost. Once, an owl flew low over our heads with a loud screech which gave me a nasty turn, but that was all. Well, not quite all. It was shortly after half past twelve when I fancied that I could detect a very slight movement towards the edge of the waste land. I mentioned this to Routledge. "Where did you think that you saw it?" he asked. I pointed to a dark hollow some fifteen yards away from where we were standing. "Funny you should pick that spot," he said, "actually that is the precise place where I first saw the thing." It was odd, certainly, but hardly decisive, and although we watched for another thirty minutes nothing else happened. When, at last, we gave up the ghost, I came away with the impression that we had been on the brink of some strange experience, but I'm afraid I still felt intractably sceptical. Maybe I'm just not psychic.

Another waterfront phantom which is said to haunt the river-lip is that of Trash, the Ghost Dog of Formby shore, and there have been numerous accounts of its hair-raising activities. Otherwise known as " The Striker," because of the harsh, blood-chilling cries which some of the older folk claim to have heard it utter, and which, they will tell you, portend death or grave misfortune to those who hear them, this unpleasant ogre is said to prowl dark parts of the shore between Formby and Ainsdale. People who have met with it describe it as a gigantic, black hound with large luminous eyes. Local legend recounts how a man who lived near the coast and used often to return home at night very much the worse for drink, had the misfortune to encounter it upon one of these vinous occasions. Filled with fear and anger, he lashed at the dog with his stick, but the stick passed right through it and, fixing him with its eyes, the creature crouched down in front of him as if about to spring. The terror-stricken man fainted clean away, but when he recovered The Striker was still there, balefully staring at him. By this time the man had sobered up sufficiently to take to his heels and make a dash for it. Rumour cannot resist the moral corollary that the drunkard henceforth turned his back on the bottle and subsequently led a life blameless as that of the staunchest Alcoholic Anonymous !

Among the legions of spectres which have stalked the night-world of Liverpool's suburban dormitories, mention must be made of the Stoneycroft Horror which caused ten people to leave a house in that district. The story is told by Mrs. Birrell, a widow, who was one of the two people who actually saw the ghost. She was having a late supper with her daughter and son-in-law, Mr. and Mrs. Rex Harte, when one of the other tenants came and told them that weird creakings, groanings and footsteps were alarming the occupants of the ground-floor. Mrs. Birrell said that she would come down at once to investigate. As she was descending the stairs, there suddenly materialised in front of her a column of light which bore the vague shape of a human figure. The figure was completely transparent and after a second or so disappeared through the wall. Mrs. Birrell screamed and fainted, and at that precise moment all the lights flickered but, mercifully, did not go out. A few weeks prior to this harrowing experience, Mrs. Birrell had gone to the cellar to put some money in the gas-meter and something had brushed past her. She turned swiftly round only to find that she was the sole human thing in all that dim basement.

Rather more than a decade ago, the people of Prescot were worried by a ghost which was said to be flitting about the old stone-quarry by Delph Lane, Whiston. Whilst doing a spot of courting, a 24-year-old seaman had crashed a hundred feet to his death off an 18-inch ledge on the quarry-brink. Shortly after this tragedy, a woman who was returning from the last house at a local cinema was alarmed as she passed the pathway leading up to the quarry when she and her companion saw a man on the footpath. " There was a look about him that caused an eerie feeling to run down my spine, and when we got within half a dozen yards of him he disappeared," she afterwards explained. Crowds subsequently spent several nights " tracking " the ghost in the quarry, but nothing came of their efforts to lay it.

More recently, a ghost manifested itself in a house in Arundel Avenue, Sefton Park. The house was occupied by a doctor in those days, and his daughter told me that, being alone there at about four o'clock in the gloaming of a December afternoon, she heard the sound of a key being placed in the front door which opened and was then gently closed. Thinking it was her father returning early from his round, she called out, but received no answer. She went downstairs : there was no one there, but as she was ascending again to her room, she felt an ice-cold wind pass over her and, although she saw nothing, a palpable presence pushed past her on the staircase. I may say that the doctor's daughter is well-known to me personally and that I can vouch for the fact that she is not an imaginative type.

Throughout the fourth fit I shall be following the phantom footsteps across the Mersey—I almost wrote The Styx—into some weird byways of Wirral.

THE FOURTH AND FINAL FIT

WEIRD HAPPENINGS IN WIRRAL

Rolling out the barrel is generally a hilarious process, unless, of course, it happens to be a ghost that is doing the rolling ! In the present instance, the presence of a spirit outside instead of inside the barrel had a distinctly dampening effect on all concerned.

The house to which the following narrative refers is an old one situated in Birkenhead, and the floor of one of its attics is sullied with the dirty crimson flush of blood. This bloodstain is said to bear witness to a horrible murder which is alleged to have taken place in that attic many years before when the house was tenanted by priests. According to the legend, one of these priests was brutally killed there, and his corpse stuffed into a barrel, prior to its being secretly disposed of. A lady who subsequently lived in the house had many strange experiences there and came to the conclusion that there was a ghastly amount of truth in the tradition. Several times, just as the grand-father-clock on the landing struck three, this lady and her two sisters were wakened by a thunderous knock. Intense silence followed, and then, from the very top of the house, there came a heavy rolling noise, horribly suggestive of the trundling of a barrel. Flight by flight, the thing bumped blindly down the stairs, pausing briefly at each landing, until the echoes of its bumpings grew fainter and fainter as it reached the cellar.

Another recently-revived story of a Wirral haunting tells of a phantom which flits through the premises of Oldershaw Grammar School at Wallasey. The ghost, according to Mr. James F. Ford of Cliff Road, Wallasey, who has recently retired after being a master at the school since it first opened way back in 1920, is that of Hubert Mayo, the school's first headmaster, who died in 1921. Mr. Alexander McGraw, now also retired after thirty-one years as art master at Oldershaw, is one of those who had an eerie experience there.

" There is one night at the school I shall never forget," he said, " although it happened all of thirty years ago." He had gone back to the school shortly after ten o'clock to frame some pictures which his pupils had painted, and did not leave the woodwork room until about half-past eleven at night. As he was closing the door behind him, he distinctly heard a rustle in the corridor like the swish of a master's gown. The passage was pitch-black, and when he got downstairs, Mr. McGraw stopped and listened, but all was still. It was a woman cleaner who actually saw the ghost one winter evening when she was filling ink-wells near Mr. Mayo's old study. The figure flitted past a room which had a stone balcony and to which there was no access. Terrified, she dropped a large ink-pot and fled in search of the caretaker who at once went round the school with a loaded revolver searching and locking all the rooms. He found no one.

Cutting across to the far side of the Wirral Peninsula, the serious ghost-seeker lights upon Thurstaston Hall, a magnificent old residence dating back to 1400, which is indisputably subject to periodic hauntings. The Thurstaston apparition is that of a woman who once owned the hall and was the last of her line to live there. She seems to have succeeded to its ownership by means of murder, for this woman confessed on her death-bed to having killed a little boy who was the real heir in order to secure the property for herself. Her guilt-seared shade manifested itself to a noted portrait-painter, Reginald Easton, who, on one occasion when the house was full, was put in the room where, more than a hundred years before, the murder was committed. He was told nothing of the ghost and retired to bed in all innocence. He awoke, however, in the small hours to find an elderly woman standing at the foot of his bed, wringing her hands and staring down at the floor as though searching for something. Not at first realizing that she was a phantom, Easton spoke to her, whereupon, after pulling the bell-rope, the woman vanished. The next day he told his host what had happened and heard the whole story of the murder. That night, Mr. Easton, who does not seem to have been afflicted with nerves, waited up for the old woman with his sketch-block by his side. She returned punctually, and continued to do so throughout the artist's stay. During her brief visits, Easton managed to complete a drawing of her, and when, afterwards, he showed it to one of her descendants, it was immediately recognised from the close resemblance it bore to a portrait of the murderess which had formerly hung in Thurstaston Hall but which had been removed thence three generations before and had never been seen by Mr. Easton.

Leasowe Castle is another ancient Wirral abode with a ghostly history. Formerly the residence of the Earls of Derby, the castle subsequently passed through the hands of many families. At one stage in its varied history, it came into the possession of a man who was involved in a bitter feud with some of his neighbours. This bellicose landowner captured among his prisoners a father and son whom he locked up in a panelled room in the castle. In a frenzy of fear, the father killed his son and then committed suicide by battering his brains out on the wall. Centuries later, when the castle was converted into an hotel, guests constantly complained of seeing the father and son standing by their bedsides and had their blood chilled by dreadful screams which issued from the Oak Room. The old castle is now a Railwaymen's Convalescent Home and it looks as if the good work which is done there has placated the spirits, for there is no recent record of any untoward happenings.

Cheshire has, like Lancashire, its share of animal ghosts and boasts a somewhat less formidable phantom dog than Trash of Formby. Its existence has the unique distinction of being recorded in the minutes of Congleton Rural Council, for at a meeting of the Council, twenty odd years ago, a letter from a retired farmer was read in which the spectral dog was referred to. The letter, which complained of the condition of a certain field footpath, went on to tell how on rough, dark nights a little white dog bearing a lighted lantern in its mouth used to appear on the path and light people across the field. " It sprang from somewhere and vanished somewhere, but nobody knew where," he wrote, adding that his father had himself seen it scores of times.

Until it was pulled down in 1934, Orchard Cottage at Lower Bebington, was frequently visited by the ghost of a horse. The cottage was at one time occupied by the well-known local antiquary, Mr. E. W. Cox, Time and again, he and his family would hear at midnight the sounds of this horse galloping up to the gate and would rush out to investigate. They never saw any sign of the animal and the closest scrutiny of the ground always failed to reveal any traces of hoofmarks.

The Old Quay House at Parkgate used also to be haunted by a friendly phantom in a red cloak. The house, which at the time of the hauntings was tenanted by Henry Melling, the artist, had, at different periods of its history, done service as a prison and an inn. During the seventeenth and eighteenth centuries, Parkgate was a busy port to which came a continual stream of travellers to and from Ireland, until the shifting of the riversands put an end to the old prosperity. Hundreds of people must have waited for the coach, or for a favourable tide, in the inn, and the ghost may have been that of one of those travellers. On the other hand, it could equally well have been the shade of some former tenant or servant. It might even have been the spirit of one of the earlier prisoners. In any event, during Henry Melling's tenancy, the old lady in the voluminous red cape used to sit silently by the fire in the room occupied by Melling's invalid niece, Clara Payne. Far from being afraid, the bedridden child grew very fond of the gentle ghost, and when the visits suddenly ceased she was missed as keenly as any flesh-and-blood friend.

The nearby village of Neston has a striking story of the mysterious advent of the ghost of a priest who appeared to Teresa Higginson, the famous Merseyside mystic. Miss Higginson, an extremely pious woman, was staying at Neston, and during the absence of the parish priest she took charge of the keys of the Roman Catholic church. Early one morning, a strange priest came to her and intimated without speaking that he wished to say mass in the church. Accordingly, she accompanied him there, unlocked the door and remained in the church with him, hearing mass and receiving Holy Communion from his hands. At the end of the ceremony, Miss Higginson followed the priest into the vestry, only to find it quite empty. The vestments had been neatly folded away but of the celebrant there was not the slightest sign. Thoroughly mystified, Miss Higginson related what had happened to the parish priest upon his return, and he consulted his Bishop. His Lordship recognised the stranger from Miss Higginson's description as a former incumbent whose body had lain buried for many a year in Neston Parish Churchyard.

But the Wirral visitation which affected the largest number of people was undoubtedly that of the Tranmere Terror, which gave the population of Tranmere a week of unrivalled fear. It began one morning when a road watchman reported that his night had been rendered decidedly unpleasant by the sudden appearance of a " gibbering face " which leered into his box from the blackness beyond his brazier. He had, he said, seen no body, and the hideous face seemed to float in the air. By the end of the day, the story had got a solid grip on the public imagination and a first-rate " scare " had developed. When darkness fell, hundreds of people were afraid to venture farther than their own doorsteps and there were almost hourly reports of the apparition's having been seen in one or other of a score of murky alleyways. The scare lasted for about a week, and then stopped abruptly as it had begun. It was never satisfactorily explained, and there are to this day those who will recount with a shudder the tale of that week when the devil came to the suburbs of Birkenhead !

* * * *

What, then, does this short survey of Haunted Merseyside amount to ? What does it prove ?

Footsteps, whisperings, the apparitions which other people claim to have seen and heard—that is not enough.

Time and again, I have gone on a ghost-hunt to this or that allegedly haunted house : always, I have arrived hopeful ; always, I have been assured that *this* time it is the real thing ; but always, I have left disappointed—a man who would like to believe in ghosts and who is open to be convinced. . . .

*IN which a Liverpool poet and his
true love make for themselves a
seventh-story heaven in the
demesne of Mammon.*

A POET IN DOCKLAND

ASTRAY one summer's evening in the stilled heart of Liverpool's
dockland, I spent a fruitful half-hour gazing into space. Space and
time, for the portion of space which riveted my gaze was a bare
plot of land at the cobbled terminus of South John Street whereon,
until a decade-and-a-half ago German bombs ploughed its bricks back
into the earth, there stood a tall dark warren of offices called Trafford
Chambers. Sixty-eight years ago an alien songbird came to nest in
the attics of that drear stronghold of nineteenth-century commerce
in the person of Liverpool's greatest native poet—Richard Le
Gallienne.

Richard Le Gallienne, poet, essayist, lion of the romantic nineties,
and son of John Gallienne, one-time secretary of the Birkenhead
Brewery Company, first saw the light of day in Everton on January
20th, 1866. Reared in Birkenhead, schooled at Liverpool College,
apprenticed to accountancy in the Fenwick Street offices of Messrs.
Chalmers & Wade, it was Le Gallienne's destiny to clamber out of the
hated rut of life behind the dead wood of a provincial office desk.
There was to be for him a brief high noon of glory as the comrade and
equal of such splendid suns of *fin de siècle* London as Oscar Wilde,
Aubrey Beardsley and Max Beerbohm, followed by a thirty-four-
year winter of discontent in stream-lined America before, conforming
to the tradition of his cohort, he returned to Europe to keep, at the
age of eighty-one, a long-postponed appointment with death.

★ ★ ★ ★

It was towards the end of 1889 that Le Gallienne, having quarrelled with the rigid puritanism of his father's home, moved into the
large well-lighted room which, for ten pounds a year, he rented on
the seventh story of Trafford Chambers. He was to remain there

little more than a year, but those twelve months were to be counted among the happiest of his whole life, and many, many times he was to look back with poignant nostalgia to that humble den at the very mast-head of that dingy building, rising high above the loftiest yards and riggings of the nearby docks, in which he " commenced author."

Le Gallienne himself has embalmed the memory of his seventh-story heaven in one of his prose fancies published in the seventh volume of that peerless nineties chronicle—*The Yellow Book.* The piece is touchingly dedicated : " For M. Le G., a Birthday Present ; 25 September, 1895," and is a sad little offering to Mildred, his first wife, who had died of typhoid in May 1894, less than three years after their marriage. Richard Le Gallienne was to marry twice more, but he never really recovered from the loss of Mildred, the little blue-eyed girl who had waited upon him at Miss MacPherson's café in Tithebarn Street, where in his clerking days he used to go for lunch.

How good life had seemed to Richard and Mildred when, after the long climb up all those dreary flights of stairs which led from the chill region of empty, echoing offices, they opened the door which hid a gracious and strangely contrasting little world of books and flowers. Cosy behind its muslin curtains, they were free to dream : he of success as a great poet ; she of becoming his wife and making a beautiful home for him and for their children. On just such nights as this the lovers would sit up there together. Sometimes Mildred would play to him upon the piano, procured with daring extravagance on hire-purchase, and softly sing, one after another, his favourite songs. At other times she would just sit quietly on the sofa watching his raven head bent over his desk as he penned page after page of his critical appreciation of George Meredith which was written in that vanished attic. And sometimes, for even poets must eat, she would cook him a meal of fried sausages, and with, if they happened to be flush, a bottle of wine between them, there they would sit, hand-in-hand, the lamp lowered, watching the stars rush down upon them through the skylight which hung above the tiny table.

Sixty-two years ago Le Gallienne wrote : " That seventh-story heaven once more leads a dull life as the office of a ship-chandler, and harsh voices grate the air where Beauty sang. The books and the flowers and the lovers' faces are gone for ever. I suppose the stars are the same, and perhaps they sometimes look down through that roof-window, and wonder what has become of those two lovers who used to look up at them so fearlessly long ago."

★　　★　　★　　★

So did I gaze, not vacantly, into space, and as evening came softly over the Mersey I saw those self-same stars sequining the curtains of night. Maybe, somewhere beyond them, Richard and his Mildred were together again at last. Maybe they were looking down on this little plot of remembered earth, for surely " there is no place where a great dream has been dreamed that is not thus watched over by the guardian angels of memory."

60. WIGAN'S KIDNAPPED CORPSE

This is a true story of a 74-year-old mystery which started with the death of an earl in Italy, and, after a gruesome little interlude in the wilds of Scotland, reached a satisfactory conclusion in the peace and quiet of Wigan Parish Church. It is the story of an attempt to traffic in a grisly merchandise—an attempt that failed !

Death is usually the end of the chapter ; in this case it was only the beginning of a series of incidents so bizarre that they captured the interest and imagination of all Britain.

On December 13th, 1880, the 25th Earl of Crawford, who was also the 8th Earl of Balcarres, died in Florence. In accordance with family tradition, it was decided that his body should be laid to rest in his native land, so the corpse was delivered into the hands of a Florentine chemist who embalmed it in preparation for its long journey back to Scotland.

After embalming, the body was placed in a shell of soft Italian wood : this was encased in lead and the two coffins were then placed in a third of carved oak embellished with chased silver fittings.

Finally, the triple coffin was enclosed in a massive sarcophagus of rich walnut wood upon the top of which was carved a huge cross. Then began the grim Odyssey ; a slow and difficult progress across the Alps, a cross-Channel voyage during a gale so heavy that the coffin had to be lashed to the deck, and on by train to Scotland.

It was on Christmas Eve, 1880, that the body reached Aberdeen. There a hearse was waiting to transport it to the late earl's Scottish estate, Dunecht House, where it was to be interred in the newly-erected Mortuary Chapel.

It must have been a weird scene at the station as the men struggled to lift the coffin, which weighed something over half a ton, into the funeral-carriage, especially when it was discovered that the hearse was not large enough to accommodate its monstrous burden, and they had to set to, there and then, to remove the outer sarcophagus.

At last, as dusk began to fall, the task was accomplished ; the hearse moved slowly off and was soon lost to sight amid the whirling snow-flakes which all but blinded the driver as he picked a careful way between the stark, frosted hedges lining the tortuous lanes to Dunecht.

The funeral took place five days later, and the earl's remains were reverently laid to rest in the granite fastness of the new mausoleum.

At the conclusion of the service, the mourners, ascending the short flight of eight steps which led up from the vault and watching the four great slabs of granite which sealed the entrance being lowered into place, little dreamed that the melancholy scene they had witnessed was destined to be the prelude to an event which was to cause a thrill of nation-wide horror.

Who, indeed, could possibly have guessed that the peace of that remote crypt was, within a few short months, to be so rudely shattered as to make it the focal point of the attention of the entire English-speaking world.

The first dark hint that all was not well in the vault came on one fine Sunday morning in May 1881. As the housekeeper was returning from the kirk that day, she became aware of a strong aromatic odour which appeared to emanate from the tomb.

The following day, the gardener also noticed this peculiar smell, but, concluding that it came from some wreaths, backed with *arbor vitae*, which lay in withered sympathy upon the dead man's grave, he did not give the matter very much thought.

In the succeeding days, however, the odour became increasingly pronounced and, as a result of this, the entrance to the crypt was examined and it was found that there was a fissure between two of the outer stones.

Workmen were summoned, the hole was filled in with lime, and there the matter would have ended had it not been for a curious communication which, on September 8th, 1881, was laid upon the desk of Mr. William Yeats, the Crawford family lawyer, at Aberdeen.

This letter bore the Aberdeen postmark and read as follows :—

> " *Dear Sir,*
> *The remains of the late Earl of Crawford are not beneath the chapel at Dunecht as you believe, but were removed hence last spring, and the smell of decayed flowers ascending from the vault since that time will, on investigation, be found to proceed from another cause than flowers.*   NABOB."

After making various enquiries, Mr. Yeats, apparently reassured, dismissed the matter as a practical joke. At the beginning of December 1881, however, the whole affair was brought suddenly and forcibly back into Yeats's mind when some labourers who were working on repairs at Dunecht House summoned him from Aberdeen in respect of an obvious disturbance of the soil covering the vault entrance.

Upon his arrival, Yeats discovered three sets of footprints in the earth and saw a number of spades, picks and other tools scattered about within the railings which guarded the approach to the mausoleum.

He also observed that one of the slabs had been moved and was now propped up some fifteen or sixteen inches by means of a piece of wood.

Without further ado, Yeats sent for the police. When they arrived they opened the vault, and, descending into it, stumbled upon a scene of nightmare disorder.

The floor was littered with a mixture of sawdust and wood-shavings which gave off the sickly-sweet fragrance which had previously been noted. The coffins stood in a row, their lids ripped off. They were all empty.

The investigators were glad to escape from that gloomy charnel-house into the fresh air. But they emerged puzzled, for nowhere in all that desecrated tomb could they discover the body of the earl: it had completely vanished.

An intensive search was immediately instituted. Bloodhounds and even clairvoyants were employed, but it was all to no avail. At his wits end, Yeats tried putting an advertisement in the Press:

" Nabob. Please communicate."

Nothing happened. A second appeal was inserted, baited this time with the offer of £50 reward. Ten days later, on December 23rd, 1881, the Earl of Crawford's London solicitors received another letter from " Nabob."

The mysterious correspondent said that he knew the where-abouts of the earl's body but was not disposed to reveal it for fear of being " assinated by rusarectionests."

The weeks turned into months and still the whole affair remained shrouded in mystery, until on July 17th, 1882, an Aberdeen rat-catcher-cum-poacher, named Charles Soutar, was arrested as the result of information laid against him by one George Machray, a game-keeper.

Soutar admitted that he was " Nabob," but persistently denied having had any hand in the abduction of the earl's body.

He told a strange story. He had been poaching near Dunecht House at about 11 o'clock one night at the end of April 1881, he said, when four men had set upon him. Levelling a pistol at his head, one of them had warned him, " Mark this ; you're known to our party, and if you breathe a syllable of what you have seen, I will have your life if you are on the face of the earth."

He was then told " Get out," and did so as fast as he could. Overcome with curiosity, he later returned to the spot where he had been assailed.

The men had disappeared, but he noticed a mound of earth where none had been before. Investigating this, he had found to his horror that it contained the body of a man, wrapped in a blanket, and emit-ting a strange fragrance.

Terrified by what he had seen, he rushed back to Aberdeen, his mind filled with the thought that murder had been done. Remembering the threat of vengeance, he had tried to forget his unpleasant adventure, but a chance meeting with a plasterer named Cowie, at the cattle show in July, had brought it all back to him when the latter happened to mention to him the curious effluvium which was issuing from the Crawford vault. He had then put two and two together and had written the " Nabob " letters.

Having heard this remarkable story, the police went at once to Dunecht and at midnight seventeen of them surrounded the plantation known as Dumbreck Wood which Soutar had described. A thorough search was made with iron probes and by 11-30 the next morning the earl's body had been discovered.

Charles Soutar was subsequently arraigned at the bar of the High Court of Justiciary, Edinburgh. He pleaded not guilty, but after a trial which lasted a day and a half he was found guilty and sentenced to five years penal servitude.

So, the strange case of the kidnapped corpse came to an end. Many people were inclined to think that Soutar was not really guilty, or that, if he were, he had played only a minor part in a drama which was the product of a much higher intelligence.

Whoever conceived and carried out this ghoulish felony, the motive at least is clear—it was for money, and was probably inspired by the recollection of how, in 1878, the corpse of an American millionaire had been snatched from its grave and held to ransom for £25,000.

Ultimately, the body of the 25th Earl of Crawford and Balcarres was reinterred, not in the Dunecht crypt of which he had planned to be the first occupant, but in the family vault beneath the Lindsay Chapel in the beautiful parish church of Wigan, where, to this day, his much-travelled corpse rests happily undisturbed.

HE SAVED LIVERPOOL FROM THE BLACK DEATH

You will find the bare bones of one of the strangest and most dramatic incidents of recent Liverpool medical history embalmed between the dusty grey covers of the Medical Officer of Health's official report for the year 1916. If you turn to page 14 of that rather drab volume you will discover the following :

" On September 25th, a labourer (aged 56 years) who lived in E—— Street and worked in a grain warehouse at the Docks became unwell. A doctor called in on the following day, suspecting plague, reported the case to the Medical Officer of Health by telephone, the house was visited, and the suspicion confirmed. The man and his wife were removed for isolation. The patient died on September 28th, but his wife did not develop the disease."

It does not make very exciting reading that flat, factual statement, and yet . . . well, listen to the story behind that soberly-commemorated tragedy.

On a winter's evening in 1915 a group of doctors who were members of the Liverpool Medical Institution met to attend a discourse in the lecture theatre of the old institution building at the top of Mount Pleasant. The meeting was a lively one and in the course of the discussion which followed the lecture a well-known Liverpool surgeon, George Palmerston Newbolt, was mercilessly ribbed because he had operated for hernia on a woman who was in reality suffering from bubonic plague. To the layman such a mistake may seem well-nigh incredible, but the fact of the matter is that the characteristic swellings or " buboes " of the plague can, when present in that part of the lower abdomen where rupture swellings most commonly occur, quite easily be confused with the physical symptoms of hernia. This confusion is especially likely to arise in a place like Liverpool where you would not normally expect to encounter the usually tropical plague. In any event, the late Mr. Newbolt *did* make the mistake and when, on this particular evening, he was forcefully reminded of it he well and truly lost his temper.

Among those present at the meeting was a young doctor who had but recently qualified and hopefully put up his plate in a suburb of this city. He listened intently to the tale of Mr. Newbolt's indiscretion and the spectacle of that eminent gentleman's embarrassment lingered with him for many a day afterwards, along with the determination that he must never fall into a similar error. Fantastic as it may seem, less than twelve months were to elapse before the long arm of coincidence was to present this young doctor with an opportunity of putting his resolve to the test.

One September morning in 1916 he received a call from a lady who told him that her husband was very poorly. When he arrived at the house the doctor found the man running a high temperature and complaining of a general feeling of malaise. He examined the patient carefully but could find no symptoms upon which to base any satisfactory diagnosis. After about a quarter of an hour, the doctor decided that the best thing to do was to wait a day or so to see if any more definite signs developed which would establish the nature of the ailment. It was just as he was turning to leave the room that the sick man called him back and said :

" Oh, by the way, doctor, I've got a queer swelling at the top of my leg. I don't know if that may have anything to do with the trouble."

As the doctor bent to examine the leg his mind suddenly went back to that evening at the Medical Institution, and when, a moment or two later, he rose from the bedside it was with the curiously strong conviction that he was faced with a case of the plague.

" What is your work ? " asked the doctor.

" I'm a stevedore at the docks," came the reply.

" Do you ever come across any rats ? "

" Yes, often. Funnily enough, I tripped over a dead one only the other day," said the patient.

The doctor's heart gave a jump. That clinched it. It *must* be the plague. For bubonic plague, the terrible Black Death which ravaged Europe in the seventeenth-century and accounted for the deaths of something like 70,000 people in London in 1665, is a disease of rats and it is conveyed to man by the bites of two species of fleas which inhabit the rat's fur. The flea bites the sick rat and if, subsequently, it bites a man it conveys the infection to him.

The disease bacteria thrive in the blood of the black rat. This creature is no longer commonly found in this country where it has, since about 1788, been gradually replaced by the brown rat, but it sometimes reaches our shores by way of rat-infested ships which come here from foreign parts.

The doctor said nothing to either the man or his wife of his terrible suspicions, but within a matter of minutes after leaving the house he was on the telephone to the Medical Officer of Health. He was, as we have said, relatively recently qualified and his statement that he thought he had a case of plague on his hands was greeted not only with friendly incredulity but with roars of laughter. Nevertheless, the possibility, however remote-seeming, was so serious a one that the ever-vigilant health department lost no time in sending another doctor to the house to investigate.

The health-department doctor, having examined the patient, inserted a syringe into the swelling and drew off a quantity of the fluid which it contained. This liquid was carefully sealed in two small bottles, one of which was sent to the city laboratories and the other despatched to London. Within a matter of hours the reply came back from the Liverpool laboratory, " *Pasteurella pestis* present " and shortly after this the discovery of the plague bacillus in the fluid contained in the second bottle was confirmed by the bacteriologists in London.

As stated in the Medical Officer of Health's report, the man was isolated at once, and the local authorities went into action immediately at the docks, where several dead rats, their blood a teeming reservoir of the sub-visible assassins, were found. All refuse was removed, the warehouse was thoroughly cleaned and disinfected, every rat run was permanently blocked and the dreadful possibility of the spread of the disease was mercifully averted. Just how fortunate was our escape can only be appreciated by those who have seen the disastrous results of an epidemic. Western Europe has been virtually free of plague since the middle of the eighteenth-century, but it continues a serious menace in places like India where, with plague mortality figures breasting the 10,000,000 mark between 1896 and 1918, the sight of doomed men and women death-pocked with its spreading black spots is all too tragically common. Remembering these things, it is awful to contemplate the panic and desolation which might so easily have fallen upon Liverpool on that sunny September day thirty-nine years ago.

And what of the doctor whose brilliant diagnosis and prompt action probably saved our city ? He is still alive—that is why his name must remain secret—still in harness ; a general practitioner, one of the unsung heroes of medicine ; still saving people from the less spectacular, but no less deadly, diseases which are the everyday plagues of modern life.

THE FABULOUS NATIONAL

Every March, the month of the lion and the lamb, sees Liverpool the brief focal point of the world's eyes. In cars and trains, in ships and aeroplanes, the great sporting world descends upon us : quiet bars hum to the rich brogues of Ireland, the drawling voices of the south and a host of unaccustomed accents. In their thousands they come, the aristocrats and the mountebanks, the race-lovers and the gamblers, and through the grey industrial pattern of our streets is woven a temporary filament of the rainbow. Whispered tips are in abundance. They may be sought in the feathered brilliance of a Monolulu or in the less conspicuous, but often more convincing, horsy shabbiness of a horde of knowledgeable, checked, booted and breeched tipsters. All is bustle and excitement for there is abroad the perennial spirit of the greatest steeplechase in the world.

But if it is upon the course at Aintree that the mounting tide of tension reaches its climax in a noisy, all-submerging wave, its presence is still felt in the lesser currents that surge and eddy through the quieter streets of sedately distant suburbs, where the usually cautious permit themselves the rare indiscretion of their annual " little flutter " upon what seems to them to be their own particular race. And is it not only proper that we should take a pride in our Grand National, for, not only is it a race of noble tradition, but it is the oldest annual steeple-chase in the world.

Although the " Sport of Kings," in its classic, flat-racing form, has been in favour since such remote times as the Greek Olympiads of 600 B.C., steeplechasing, or wildgoose chasing, is of much more recent origin.

It all started in Ireland in 1752, when a certain Mr. Edmund Blake accepted a Mr. O'Callaghan's challenge to decide the relative merits of two hunters by means of a cross-country horse-race to be run over the $4\frac{1}{2}$ miles which separated the church of Buttevant from the spire of St. Leger's church at Doneraile in County Cork. As the St. Leger steeple was visible throughout, the match was facetiously dubbed a " Steeplechase." The idea of making wagers upon the prowess of their favourite hunters soon caught on among Irish hunting-men and by 1825 regular steeplechases were being run for prizes of plates, and it was not long before the framing of various restrictions

79

upon riders and weights elevated steeplechasing to the position of a recognized sport.

Steeplechasing made its first appearance in England in 1830 as a result of a suggestion made during a dinner by some officers of the Household Cavalry to the landlord of the Turf Hotel at St. Albans. The landlord, an astute man named Tom Coleman, saw the benefit which an annual steeplechase at St. Albans would be to him and promptly set about instituting it. His foresight was amply rewarded, for not only did he earn for himself the title of "The Father of Steeplechasing " but he also managed to add considerably to his income by letting his rooms at a guinea a night at racing time.

Of course Coleman had many imitators among the hotel-keeping fraternity, but the most successful of these was William Lynn of the Waterloo Hotel at Aintree. He, with an eye to his bank balance, entered into an arrangement with his farmer neighbours whereby they agreed to allow an annual steeplechase over their land and, on the 29th February, 1836, the first Liverpool Steeplechase was run at Maghull.

Lynn's meetings continued annually until 1839, when a syndicate was formed which purchased the racing amenities from him. This year saw at Aintree the establishment of the first proprietary course ever organised, and it was here, on the 26th February, 1839, that the Grand Liverpool Steeplechase, the first Grand National proper, was run.

The day dawned fine and spring-like, with just a slight breeze blowing up from the Mersey. The course was crowded with spectators who would look strange to our twentieth-century eyes. The men wore top-hats and frock-coats for the main part, although there would still be some who favoured the already old-fashioned Hessian boots and knee-breeches. The women were all shawls, voluminous skirts and large fan-like bonnets. The seventeen runners got off to a good start although the going was to be hard for it had been a real fill-dyke February. The race abounded in incidents. At this time the course was run over unflagged, brook-studded ploughland and one of the horses, " Rust," was trapped in a lane by a hostile crowd who were determined that he should not win ! Another, " Dictator," fell at the first brook, was remounted by his jockey, Carlin, only to drop dead at the next fence.

But the most famous incident of all was the christening of Becher's Brook. The gentleman whose name was bestowed on this obstacle was Captain Becher, son of a Norfolk farmer and horse-dealer. Bred in an atmosphere of horses, he was early introduced to the saddle, a position which he showed a regrettable tendency to abandon throughout his life, for he was renowned for the number and variety of his falls ! He was the tumbler *par excellence,* and in many an old racing-print he is depicted in the act of falling. Becher was a member of the old school of gentlemen riders who lived the life of a professional jockey travelling from meeting to meeting, often sleeping on horseback, until his thick, curled beard (which the wags said added to his weight in the saddle) became a familiar sight to race-goers everywhere. In this first National the Captain was riding " Conrad " and as they came up to the brook at which he was to tumble into immortality the horse stumbled. Becher took a header into the water, wherein he wisely sought refuge from the flurry of skull-splintering hoofs. As soon as the danger was past, the sporting Captain sprinted after " Conrad," leapt into the saddle and set off at a cracking pace in pursuit of the field. He got as far as Valentine's Brook, where he was again thrown, and " Conrad," having had enough, made certain that the Captain should not catch him a second time !

The first man to win the Blue Riband of 'chasing was Jem Mason who rode " Lottery " first past the post in 1839. Jem was the son of a Stilton horse-jobber. He had schooled horses, including " Lottery," for John Elmore and had long dreamed of becoming a famous jockey and marrying his master's daughter with whom he was in love. He was one of the lucky ones and his dreams came true. The amazing thing about this man and the horse upon which he rode in so many Nationals is that they hated each other and Jem was always obliged to conceal his Elmore blue racing-jacket under his coat until he was mounted.

The next race was run on March 5th, 1840, and was won by " Jerry," but because of the winning of a wager made by a Mr. Power, the owner-rider of a horse named " Valentine," it is often, somewhat unfairly, referred to as " Valentine's National." For the second National, Lord Sefton had caused a new stone wall to be erected and Mr. Power had made a rather rash bet that he would be the first over it. Off went the field of twelve, " Valentine " like an arrow from the bow, thundering to the Canal Turn which he negotiated safely. But he went at the next brook as though it had not been there, and it was only by a magnificent display of aerial acrobatics and the execution of a miraculous corkscrew-like twist that he managed to land on the far side of what was to be known henceforth as " Valentine's Brook." The gallant horse went on to lead the field over the new wall and win his master's wager, although he lost his lead subsequently and finished third to " Jerry."

The year 1841 is noteworthy in that the race was won for the first time by a mare, the valiant "Charity." Since then only a dozen other " remarkable ladies " have finished first in this most arduous of races :—" Miss Mowbray " (1852), " Anatis " (1860), " Jealousy " (1861), " Emblem " (1863), " Emblematic " (1864), " Casse Tête " (1872), " Empress " (1880), " Zoedone " (1883), " Frigate " (1889), " Shannon Lass " (1902), " Sheila's Cottage " (1948) and " Nickel Coin " (1951). It is interesting to recall in passing that it was in the year of " Frigate's " win that Mrs. Maybrick and her husband had that quarrel upon the Aintree course which was among the first causes of the murder for which she later stood trial and which became Liverpool's criminal *cause célèbre* of 1889.

In 1842 the National was won by Tom Olliver on " Gaylad." Tom Olliver was another Aintree character of the calibre of Captain Becher and Jem Mason. " Black Tom," as he was popularly called, was a native of Angmering in Sussex, who had been, in his own words " born and bred hopelessly insolvent." He was brought up by his uncle, Page of Epsom, who taught him his three R's—reading, writing and riding ! When the stable passed from Page, the young Tom went to Ireland, whence he returned to Liverpool several years later with only a few coppers in his pocket. He found a job schooling horses and eventually graduated to jockeyship. His National career was a distinguished one. He finished second on " Seventy-Four " in the 1839 race and besides winning in 1842 he also won on " Vanguard " in 1843 and on " Peter Simple " in 1853, a record of wins exceeded only by that of George Stevens, the Grand National horseman of all time, who, from running away from his home at Cheltenham to become a stable-boy, lived to achieve the distinction of winning the National five times between 1856 and 1870. By 1855, Tom Olliver was riding in his seventeenth consecutive National and his Aintree career came to an end in 1859 when he was thrown by " Claudius " his last National mount.

Upon the eve of the race in 1847 a very curious happening took place. A clairvoyance act was in progress at a Liverpool theatre and the mediumistic lady was asked by a National-minded audience to give them the winner of the morrow's 'chase. After a suitable period of concentration the clairvoyant uttered her prophecy in favour of " Matthew." And the unbelievable happened, " Matthew " won ! He was the first Irish-bred horse to win the National, which since 1900 alone has been won by more than thirty horses whose bone and substance has been built out of the rich, limestone soil of Ireland. Among the notable " foreigners " who have jumped to victory must be mentioned " Rubio " (1908) the first American-bred horse to win the National, which has since been won by another American, " Battleship," in 1938, with Bruce Hobbs up. Hobbs was, incidentally, only seventeen years old and the youngest jockey ever to taste the fruits of a National victory. France sent the 1909 winner, " Lutteur III."

The achievement of the lady fortune-teller in 1847 was certainly unique in the history of the Grand National, for it has always been, more than any other, a completely unpredictable race. Indeed, it is often and aptly described as " anybody's race ! " Time and time again there have been odd and unexpected winners. Among those horses whose names are inscribed upon the equine Roll of Honour are many with the most fantastic histories. " Emigrant " (1857) was once won on a game of cards ; " Salamander " (1866) was bought from a poor Irish family for £35 and won stakes to the tune of some £29,750 ; " Roquefort " (1885) once drew a dogcart ; " Grudon " won with butter in his shoes, to prevent him from slipping in the snow in the white National of 1901 ; " Rubio " (1908) had drawn an hotel bus in America ; " Glenside " (1911) was a one-eyed horse ; " Poethlyn " (1918 and 1919) had been sold to a publican for £17 ; " Master Robert " (1924) once worked in a plough, while " Tipperary Tim " (1928) won with a tube in his throat. In 1904 the laurels went to a stout-hearted horse, " Moifaa," who had swum ashore when his ship had been wrecked in British waters.

And if the stories of some of the horses seem strange, the race itself has seen many events hardly less queer in its time. Victory has repeatedly been thrown to the lucky horse by the hand of chance, and often it has been the others' lack of luck that has proved a blessing to the winner. Such was the case back in 1872 when Casse Tête won the day. Again in 1877, it was upon the wings of good fortune that " Austerlitz " won his one and only National. Some horses seem to have a natural liking for Aintree, whilst others, among them the 1934 winner, " Golden Miller," hailed as the horse of the century, appear to take a strong dislike to it.

This is hardly to be wondered at, for the race is probably the most gruelling in the world. The course is a double circuit totalling 4 miles 856 yards. On the first round the horses have to clear sixteen jumps, and on the second, fourteen. The existing time record for this stiff 'chase was set by " Reynoldstown " in 1935 when he completed the course in 9 minutes 20⅕ seconds. In 1846, due to a mistake in flagging, the course was involuntarily extended to nearly five miles. This longest National ever was won by " Pioneer."

" Reynoldstown," the record-maker, is one of that elect equine company who have brought off a double victory (1935, 1936) in which he equalled the achievement of " Abd-El-Kader " (1850, 1851), " Peter Simple " (1849, 1853), " The Colonel " (1869, 1870) who was later to become Kaiser Wilhelm the First's charger, " The Lamb " (1868, 1871) the only grey ever to win the race, " Manifesto " (1897, 1899) and " Poethlyn " (1918, 1919).

Of these, " Manifesto " has earned the title of the National horse of all time, and his was a magnificent record. He was first twice, third three times, fourth once and unplaced upon one occasion. In all these Nationals he fell only once. On his second win, in 1899, he carried the top weight of 12 stone 7 lbs, a feat in which he was rivalled by " Cloister " (1893), " Jerry M." (1912) and " Poethlyn " (1919).

In the earlier years, before the construction of a proper course, the size of the field offered few problems, but in later years it became necessary to devise a number of qualifying conditions upon the eligibility of would-be entrants. The greatest number of runners ever, was in 1929 when " Gregalach " won out of a field of 66 horses which had to be lined up in two rows. The smallest field was in " Zoedone's " year (1883) when there were only 10 starters. Of course the field is always considerably reduced by the end of the race and in 1882, 1921 and 1928 only two horses succeeded in completing the course. This led to the rather curious position that the last horse was also the second !

Up to 1941 the race had an unbroken history of 102 years, although during the First World War it abandoned its old home at Aintree and substitute races were run at Gatwick in 1916, 1917 and 1918. During the Second World War, however, there was no Grand National from 1941-1945.

And each year the excitement is renewed. Each year we hope that the race will be in the tradition of the fair weather Nationals and that it will not be a day of thick fog, as when " Wild Man From Borneo " (1895) won an all but invisible race by a length and a half, or a repetition of those conditions which, in 1858, saw the outsider " Little Charley " run to victory through snow and a half-gale in the National that had had to be postponed for three days.

What, we wonder, will be the name of *this* year's winner ? Who has not dreamed of the infallible, magic tip such as was offered to that Liverpool audience in 1847 ? Yet how many of them would, for lack of faith, have failed to benefit from it ? For us there remains but the abortive study of form, the loud claims of the tipsters, of whom there is a confident one for every horse in the race, or, and perhaps best of all, the ubiquitous pin !

For the winning owner there will be about £10,000, including a gold trophy valued at about £200. For the trainer of the winning horse there will be a cup valued at about £50 and for the jockey there will be a cup valued at about £25. And if, materially, his gain shall seem the least, he will not be discontented, for he will have fulfilled the greatest ambition of all 'chasing men. And in the slight pause, the breath-taking, before the glory breaks upon his head, he may find a quiet minute in which to grasp the outstretched, congratulatory hands of old Captain Becher, limping up from his latest fall, Jem Mason, Tom Olliver and a host of other ghosts whose sporting spirits surely haunt the deep shadows of the thorn hedges and hover about the ruffled waters of the brooks of their beloved legacy of earth at Aintree.

DEEMING THE RAINHILL DEMON

The ghastly and murderous saga of Frederick Bailey Deeming, alias Williams, alias Harry Lawson, alias Lord Dunn, self-styled Baron Swanston, self-styled Inspector of Regiments, spans two continents. It begins quietly enough with the birth of a son to a Birkenhead tinsmith in the 1840's, and ends, after a fearful crescendo of murder, in which at least six harmless people lost their lives, on the gallows at Melbourne, Australia, on May 23rd, 1892.

On July 21st, 1891, a stranger alighted from a train at Rainhill and took a room at the Railway Station Hotel. The man, who signed the register as Williams, was about fifty years of age, good-looking in a hard, masculine sort of way, with light-coloured hair, a fair moustache and a stocky, though well-built, body. It was not long before he let it be known among his bar-parlour acquaintances that he was an Inspector of Regiments—a government appointment which appeared to involve a great deal of travelling about and put him on terms of intimacy with all the most important people in the British Empire—and that he was due in a very short time to retire on a princely pension.

Among those who listened with open-mouthed respect to Mr. Williams's tales, none was more impressed than the landlord of the Railway Station Hotel, and it was to him that Williams confided that he was really remaining in the district as a favour to an old friend of his, Baron Brook, who had begged him to find for him a modest but comfortable house within convenient distance of Liverpool.

Now it so happened that a friend of the landlord's, a Mrs. Mather who kept the local newsagent's shop, owned just such a property as Williams seemed to be looking for, and the landlord was proud and happy to effect an introduction. Williams viewed the property—Dinham Villa—and prounced himself well-satisfied as to its entire suitability. He also viewed Mrs. Mather's pretty 25-year-old daughter, Emily. He was apparently well-satisfied with her, too, for, after the briefest of courtships, he married her.

It was during the salad days of his courtship that a rather unfortunate circumstance threatened to mar that delightful interlude for Mr. Williams A day or two after he had moved into Dinham Villa, which he was ostensibly preparing for the Baron, a cab drew up outside his handsome front door and disgorged a young woman and four children upon his well-scrubbed step. Their arrival seemed at first to have a distinctly depressing effect upon the ageing Romeo, but he rapidly recovered his usual good spirits and, indeed, made a point of telling all and sundry how nice it was to have his sister and her brood of little ones staying with him, and how lonely it would be when, after a short holiday, she would have to leave to join her husband who was abroad. As a matter of fact, the lady had no intention whatsoever of depriving Williams of the solace of her company for she was his wife.

One afternoon shortly after his " sister's " arrival, Mr. Williams paid a visit to Mrs. Mather and told her that, providing she had no objection, he proposed to make one or two trifling alterations to the villa which he felt would be necessary if the Baron was to be satisfied with his choice. He had noticed, he said, that the floorboards of most of the downstairs rooms were somewhat rough and unevenly laid, and, as the Baron was inordinately proud of a number of exceptionally fine and valuable carpets which he had collected in the course of his travels, he felt that something ought to be done to prevent the possibility of the state of the floors from damaging them. Williams added that he would himself, of course, meet all expenses incurred and explained that it was his intention to take up all the faulty boards and cement the entire surface of the ground beneath them as a precaution against damp. Needless to say, Mrs. Mather thought the idea an excellent one.

So Williams set to work with a will. From a local builder he purchased a pickaxe and several sacks of cement. Unfortunately, his " sister " was not available to help him as, according to the story he told, she had now departed for a sunnier clime. Still, he made the best of things, attending to the cementing himself and engaging a carpenter to help with the re-laying of the boards.

Once that floor was finally set in order, Williams seemed much relieved. He celebrated the completion of the work with a discreet little party. Light refreshments were served ; healths were drunk ; there was dancing across the smooth new boards, and, as the evening drew to its happy close, Williams set the seal to a merry occasion by asking Emily Mather if she would consent to become his wife. With many a pretty blush, she accepted his proposal.

No sooner was their marriage arranged, than the Baron became unaccountably awkward and decided that his pressing need for a house in the vicinity of Liverpool had ceased to exist. An apologetic Mr. Williams accordingly vacated Dinham Villa and took up his abode in Mrs. Mather's house pending the celebration of his nuptials.

A few weeks after their wedding, Williams told his bride that his duties as an Inspector of Regiments necessitated their immediate departure for Australia. There, the Williams's moved into a small furnished house at Windsor, a suburb of Melbourne, and barely had they unpacked their bags when Mr. Williams became suddenly and unaccountably dissatisfied with the state of the dining-room floor. Up came the boards, down went some cement and, by the most amazing coincidence, Mr. Williams's second wife vanished from the scene.

Practice makes perfect they say, but Williams's second attempt at floor-laying was by no means an improvement on his first. So bad a job did he make of it in fact that when, soon after his wife's disappearance, Williams left the house, the owner felt obliged to take a hand at this re-laying business himself. The results of this little essay in floor-fixing were to prove disastrous for Mr. Williams, for beneath the cement was discovered the corpse of his wife.

At the time of Mrs. Williams's resurrection her sorrowing husband was on the verge of marrying again, but the police soon put a stop to that. While he was cooling his ardour in an Australian gaol, the Melbourne police communicated with the Lancashire Constabulary who promptly made their way to Dinham Villa where they, too, embarked upon what seems to have been the ubiquitously popular pastime of pulling up the floor.

What their excavations revealed may be said to have tied the knot in the rope which was already round Williams's neck. A foot below the cement were huddled the bodies of a woman and four children. The news spread rapidly, creating a sensation paralleled only in modern times by the laying bare in Notting Hill's Rillington Place of the gruesome secrets of Christie's kitchen. It was a macabre touch that, in the ensuing rush for newspapers, as the only newsagent in the Rainhill district at that time, it was Mrs. Mather who was obliged to sell the reports of her daughter's death in Australia and of the further terrible evidence against the man she married that was being uncovered at Dinham Villa.

Meanwhile, the Sydney police recollected a similar discovery which had been made beneath the floor of a house in their city some two or three years previously, following the disappearance of another Mrs. Williams and her two children. That mystery had never been satisfactorily cleared up, and it was decided that the Mr. Williams now languishing in Melbourne Gaol was undoubtedly the author of that characteristic little piece of skulduggery too.

Frederick Deeming's trial opened on May 8th, 1892, at Melbourne Criminal Court.

Standing there in the dock, Deeming was at last occupying the position to which all his life of murder and make-believe had inexorably been leading.

The youngest of seven children, he had early disappointed his worthy, if humble, parents, by his persistent refusal to remain in any of a series of jobs which had been found for him. For a while his father had supported him in idleness, until at length he had become a steward on one of the tall ships and set forth to see the world.

For several years his family heard nothing of him, and then he suddenly reappeared bedecked with costly-looking jewellery, flashing a well-filled wallet and full of tales of the rich harvest of the South African goldfields.

He remained home just long enough to savour the envy and admiration of friends and family and then was away again.

Australia, New Zealand, South Africa and America were all ports of call in his criminous Odyssey where he managed to pick up in various shady ways the money which he required for his personal adornment, the support of a succession of brassy women friends and the satisfaction of his craving to make an impression. After many years of these fitful comings and goings, Deeming at last brought home a wife and child to meet his parents and informed them that he and his family were off to settle in Australia.

It was not long, however, before he had deserted this young wife and was off on his travels once more.

News of Deeming comes next from Europe. He stayed briefly in Antwerp, where he was known to the smart set as Lord Dunn. But some chicanery or other necessitated His Lordship's hurried departure, and it was as Harry Lawson, wealthy Australian sheep-farmer, that the protean Deeming next appeared at Beverley, near Hull.

Here, he lived in a good-class boarding-house, contrived to " marry " the proprietress's daughter, perpetrated a spectacular series of swindles on Hull jewellers, booked a passage to Montevideo and was on the high seas before his frauds were discovered.

This time he was not to escape. He was arrested when he landed at Montevideo, brought back to England and sent to prison for nine months.

Free once again, he made his way to Rainhill where, as we have seen, the wife and family he had abandoned caught up with him and were promptly murdered for their pains.

Strangely enough, Deeming was never tried for the Rainhill killings, but he was found guilty of the murder of Emily Mather at Windsor and sentenced to death.

He divided his time in gaol between considerations of his fate in this world and the next, alternately indulging in the purely practical exercise of making neat little drawings of gibbets and the reading of the Bible.

Outwardly calm and cheerful, some clue to the state of his inner feelings is afforded by the fact that during those last weeks his hair turned snow-white.

It was a lovely morning when, on May 23rd, 1892, Deeming strolled out to the scaffold, smoking a large cigar, which had been given him by the executioner, and chatting amiably with the prison officials.

Surely fate played a strange trick on him at the end when it selected Swanston Gaol as the place where the man who had so often called himself Baron Swanston was deftly despatched upon the last of his many journeys.

THE INSIDE STORY OF LIVERPOOL'S BIG BEN

Mercifully there was a lift : I had dreaded the prospect of those 483 steps.

" This way," said Mr. Corden and without another word he led me straight into the mechanical heart of England's biggest clock.

Mr. James Corden, by the way, is the Engineer at the Liver Buildings and he is also the Keeper of the Clock—the man who is responsible for Liverpool's time.

The Western Clock-Chamber into which I followed him is a large, whitewashed apartment which somehow reminded me of an outsize pigeon-loft. As soon as the little door which leads into it had been unlocked, I became aware of a curious click-clacking noise. It sounded for all the world as if a great flock of giant pigeons was interminably pecking at a wooden floor.

" That's caused by the escapement-wheels," explained Mr. Corden, wiping his hands upon the piece of cotton-waste which engineers always carry and which seems to be as beloved a professional symbol as a doctor's stethoscope. I said, " Oh, yes," and tried to look as if such horological technicalities were not utterly beyond me.

Feeling extraordinarily dwarfed, I stood in the centre of the Clock-Chamber, on three sides of which the vast, opalescent dials of Great George—that is the Liver clock's name—soared ceilingwards. The fourth clock-face reigns in splendid isolation in the Eastern tower. Seen in close-up, the dials are positively overpowering. Each measuring 25 feet in diameter, they beat London's Big Ben by a full 2½ feet. How many, one wonders, of the crowds who queue nightly within the shadow of these Gargantuan timepieces realise that the bus for which they are patiently waiting is a mere matter of twelve inches longer than the edge to edge stretch of one of those bland clock-faces ? Even stranger, is the fact that once, in the long-ago, before Great George had been hoisted to his turret top, he did service as a luncheon-table. It was to mark the achievement of Messrs. Gents, in whose Leicester workshops the remarkable piece of clockwork had been brought to life, that some forty leading lights sat themselves primly about the perimeter of one of those dials to enjoy a suitably festive luncheon-party.

Across these gigantic surfaces creep 14-foot minute-hands, unendingly circling the 48 minute-marks, each of which is separated from its neighbour by a distance of 14 inches.

"What kind of numerals are used to show the hours ?" asked the engineer suddenly.

"Roman," I replied without hesitation.

"Everyone says that," smiled Corden. "As a matter of fact the hour-marks are not numerals at all. They are just plain black lines each of which is three feet high."

Behind each clock-face is a large circle of white-distempered wall. This is the reflector and is of exactly the same size as the dial which it backs. Between this wall and the dial are hung six sodium lighting-tubes equipped with small sheets of opalescent glass. This arrangement concentrates the light onto the reflector which rediffuses it evenly through the clock-face and produces so good an effect at night that experts regard the Liver clock as one of the best illuminated in the world. At one time the efficiency of the reflectors was briefly menaced by a public who so far misunderstood their purpose as to regard them as a species of monster visitors' books. Many people apparently suffer from a Bill-Stumps-like conviction that it is required of them to leave their mark behind. Such individuals seem to descry in any expanse of bare, white wall an irresistible invitation to scrawl their names upon it. Gradually the signatures mounted, until at last they reached a height of 15 feet from the floor ! Many famous names figured among these mural graphiti, but no matter how brightly some of the names may have shone they did not compensate for the overall dimming of the reflectors which their presence produced. Now the reflectors have been redistempered and I read dismay in Mr. Corden's face as he spotted a couple of recent scribblings which had appeared on their virgin whiteness.

After that, we ascended to a narrow, iron-railed gallery which runs around the entire clock-chamber at a height of about 15 feet. Here, in glass cases, is lodged the actual mechanism of the clock. There is a separate works to each clock-face, but these are all controlled by a master-clock which is situated 200 feet below in the main entrance hall of the building. The clock is powered by electricity and runs off batteries which are trickle charged.

It is Mr. Corden's daily task to see that Great George is right. He takes his responsibility very seriously. Every morning at 10 a.m. there is a careful time-check.

"How is it done ?" echoed the Keeper of the Clock. "Simply by lifting the telephone and dialing ' TIM.' We check it again at 1 o'clock when the Birkenhead gun goes off."

Sometimes people ring up and complain that the clock is wrong. Every complaint is carefully investigated. One man kept telephoning and insisting that the clock was three minutes slow and added bitterly that for the last few nights he had missed his bus through it. On investigation it transpired that he had been craning his head out of a nearby office window and had been looking at the clock from such an angle that he got an entirely wrong impression of the position of the minute-hand. To get an accurate reading you must view the clock full on. Mr. Corden got his worst-ever fright one day when, looking up, he saw to his horror that all the faces on the Western Tower were showing different times. One dial was ten minutes slow, one fifteen minutes slow and one twenty minutes slow ! The explanation lay in the fact that a party of over fifty Dutch children, who had been allowed to visit the clock-chamber, had succumbed to the temptation to lay hands on the pendulums. Such an occurrence underlines the wisdom of the Committee of Management's ruling that all persons obtaining permission to visit the clock must now be accompanied by an official.

Actually, Mr. Corden's proudest boast is that Great George is never more than 7 seconds out, which, all things considered, is a wonderful record. Although it is scarcely possible for Corden to take his work home with him, he does his best to keep an eye on it long after the fingers of his charge have pointed the hour for his day's labours to end. Many a night he leans out from a top window of his home, three miles away in Birkenhead, and takes an affectionate peep at Great George through a telescope, " just to make sure that all is well."

It was a few minutes to five when we left the clock-chamber and made our way up a winding stone stairway to the cupola above Great George. 300 odd feet up, we came out into the strong, fresh wind which always sweeps the roof of Liverpool. Below, the city stretched like a toy town with the silver ribbon of the Mersey unwinding to the horizon. From this point the Great Orme at Llandudno is easily visible and on a clear day you can just see Blackpool Tower. In the centre of the cupola there is a kind of slate-coloured, conical stack from the top of which project eight loud-speakers, carefully protected against the vagaries of the weather by neat plastic covers. These are the veritable mouthpieces of the clock. Although Great George came to Merseyside to mark the Coronation of King George V in 1911, it was not until another Coronation Year, forty-two years later, that this marvellous turret-clock found a voice. Hitherto it has been silent because of the tremendous weight of bells which would have been necessary to give it tongue. Today, however, cumbersome bells are at a discount, their deep-throated chimes can be produced electronically. Below in the clock-chamber, there is a mysterious grey-painted cabinet in which tiny automatic hammers strike slender wires and their tinkling vibrations, amplified hundreds of times, are relayed to the loud-speakers above.

Just then there came a loud, humming, electric sort of sound through the loud-speakers.

" The chimes are warming up," commented Mr. Corden.

Although I was half expecting it, when the first chime thundered out I nearly fell off the roof with fright. In that instant I knew how Theseus must have felt when he heard the bellow of the Minotaur. The impact of the chime was like a brazen artillery firing in one's head ; it was deafening, soul-splitting : the entire tower seemed to rock. Surely, I thought, the whole of Liverpool will rush forth in terror. But not a bit of it : no one even looked up. All that happened was that some of the 3,000 people who work daily on the 40,000 square feet of the 17 floors of the towering cliff of masonry which Great George crowns, began to spill out into the streets like a dark column of worker-ants. And I just went on standing there, my ears singing in tune with the great waves of sound which kept on ringing out over the cold, wide estuary.

*A TIMELY tribute to those
battered troubadours whose sad
music tinkles to the lilt of coins.*

THE LAST TIME I MET TCHAIKOVSKY

THE last time I met Tchaikovsky we quarrelled—at least he quarrelled with me. Picking up his battered violin case and flinging it down again on the floor of Central Station café to emphasise his disgust, he brushed the crumbs from his somewhat off-white beard and said, " None of you ignorant Liverpool people appreciate music." I tried to protest. It was no use at all. " Two measly shillings in three hours," he muttered angrily and swept out to begin his second recital.

Tchaikovsky, I had better explain, was only his nickname. I never knew his real name for it did not appear on any bill-boards. He *was* a Russian and music *was* his profession, but his platform was the street corner. An old, bent man, grime-grained, in a tattered raincoat, he was one of that fast-disappearing band of troubadours who have, across the years, enlivened the Liverpool street scene with their alfresco entertainments. Now he has gone, exchanged his asthmatic old violin for, one hopes, a more tuneful harp, and his only memorial is a great silence in the grey streets where once he sent the notes chasing one another in plaintive pursuit of a few pennies. He has gone to join the other shades whose memories haunt our kerb-sides—shades like that of ' Harpo,' the little sharp-faced man in the pancake-flat cap who carried a zither before him as delicately as if it were a tray of crown Derby ; and the old man with the mammoth white moustache who, with a concertina in his hands, drumsticks on his elbows, a huge drum on his back, a pair of cymbals attached to his heel by a string, a triangle, and a mouth-organ, held by means of a sort of iron collar to his lips, was Liverpool's only one-man-band.

I doubt if in all Liverpool you could find more than half a dozen street entertainers to-day. Three of the real old-timers are still going strong. 65-year-old Harry Walker, who plays the banjo to the cinema queues and who will proudly tell you that he once did a broadcast, and Alf Morton and his partner, George, who form a musical ensemble of two with guitar and accordion. More recent recruits are one-legged Charlie 'Leggy' Norton, who strums a banjo and at the same time coaxes a tune out of a mouth-organ, and William George McMahon, a regular Saturday evening performer at Jimmy Quinn's White Star Hotel, who has these last twenty years been 'working the pubs' with his accordion.

★   ★   ★   ★

How bare the streets seem to-day when one remembers the rich past : the ballad-singers, the barrel-organs with swarthy Italians turning the handles as monkeys in little red fezzes and jackets collected the coppers ; the travelling bears which danced, or rather swayed, at the ends of their chains to the wheezings of a concertina ; colourful characters like the cannon-ball man who would throw a heavy cannon-ball up, catch it on his back and roll it dexterously around his shoulders and arms, and the negro whose usual pitch was a piece of waste land near Langton Dock—though sometimes he would appear at the top of James Street—who used to fling a coconut or turnip high into the air and allow it to fall and shatter itself on his forehead. Near Paddy's Market was the dancing-nigger man, an old negro who manipulated a wired frame on a trestle in front of him. Attached to the wires were numbers of little rag-dolls which danced up and down as he kept up a continuous chanting of " We have butter-milk all the week and whisky on a Sunday," and hammered an accompaniment on the frame with his knuckles. And outside Reynolds's Waxworks in Lime Street, you would as often as not hear the woeful wailing of the blind Irish piper.

There must be many who still remember 'Old Jakes,' a fine old chap who, with his long grey beard and a mane of hair that hung down to his shoulders, looked like a biblical prophet. Summer and winter he wore a heavy greatcoat which reached to his ankles, and his toes were clearly visible poking out of the ends of his boots. Between about 1910 and 1920 you could see him any day in the streets around the Cotton Exchange. His instrument was the harp, but it was such a harp as no one had ever played (including 'Old Jakes') for the strings were literally pieces of string, many of which had large knots in them. Naturally, the harp emitted no sound whatsoever, but ' Old Jakes ' did his best to supply the deficiency by crooning some weird tune of his own as his fingers plucked at the unresponsive strings. The wags christened him ' The Lost Chord.'

Not far away, in Pownall Square, you could find a character known as ' Hifer Stifer.' ' Hifer ' was a singer in the old ballad tradition, but his repertoire was somewhat limited. To be honest, it consisted of the chorus of one song :

Hi ! for it. Hi ! for it.
Hi ! for it still.
Hi ! for the little house
—under the hill.

This, sung over and over again, rapidly, to the accompaniment of some bells which he rattled on his wrists. How he came by the name of ' Hifer ' is painfully obvious.

*   *   *   *

Characters all, these artists of the pavements were the lineal descendants of the strolling players, wandering minstrels and troubadours who from the earliest times travelled about England. They may have been ragged, often unwashed, but they must occupy a proud place in our folklore, and there is a certain rough justice in the fact that after all the long years of neglect and slowly-falling pennies their colourful wraiths should be summoned back to the drab stage of the Liverpool streets to take a tardy curtain-call.

WHEREIN members of Liverpool's exclusive Junior Turf Club disclose the secret of the man with the £500 boot-box and many another as strange a fare.

TAXI !

A GREEN wooden hut in the centre of Williamson Square is the most exclusive café in Liverpool. It bears no sign, nothing to identify it as an eating-house. I don't suppose one person in a thousand has passed through its little green door, for this is Liverpool's last surviving cabman's shelter and in order to qualify for admittance you must be a taxi driver.

One evening recently I knocked at that small door. It was opened by Mrs. Farrimond who for nearly twenty years now has been catering for Liverpool's hungry cabbies. When I had explained to her that I wanted to meet some of the men who drive the city's taxis, she led me into a large square room and sat me down with a cup of tea at a long oilcloth-covered table round which a dozen or so taxi drivers were busy addressing themselves to huge plates of liver and bacon.

Once upon a time a visit to a cabman's shelter was an essential ingredient of a real night out. In the days of the Edwardian swells many a reveller, homeward-bound from one of those glittering parties of a vanished age, would plead for a plate of bacon and eggs or toad-in-the-hole for himself and the lovely lady on his arm. Nor was it only stage-door Johnnies with their pretty prizes from the chorus who sat down eagerly to sausage and mash in such places. In a certain shelter hard by London's Green Park, and known far and wide as the Junior Turf Club, you could regularly meet famous men like the poet, Ernest Dowson, and Sir Ernest Shackleton, the explorer, and, cheek-by-jowl with ravenous down-and-outs, gay young sprigs of the nobility. It is even whispered that from time to time the bearded face of a certain Royal Prince might be glimpsed there quaffing a cup of coffee that could not be found in a palace at 3 a.m.

* * * *

But all that is changed now. The midnight sausage has been outlawed, and to-day the cabbies' shelter has no visitors. It is a great pity because the cabby off duty is a character worth knowing. I could scarcely credit that those witty laughing men I met round Mrs. Farrimond's table were the austere figures behind whom I have so often sat in their black leather taxis. Until then, the man at the wheel had always been something of an enigma to me. I never really considered him as a human being. He was a back seen through a window— a hunched back expressing boredom or irritability, an erect back signifying alertness, even cockiness, but just a back. Sometimes I noticed his hat, whether it was a battered trilby or a smart peaked-cap. But mostly I accepted him almost as a part of his machine and only began to endow him with individuality when I started to think about how much I ought to tip him.

Now I know quite a bit about his natural history. I know that there are 300 taxis in Liverpool which operate from 102 stands, excluding those at the three main railway stations. I know that a taxi costs £1,012 to buy and that its life is exactly 11 years. I have learned that a taximeter must be bought separately, and that as it costs £55 many drivers prefer to hire one at the rate of 3s. a week. I have visited the Hackney Carriage Office in Hood Street where, before he is issued with one of the coveted metal badges, every candidate must pass an eyesight test, a special driving test and a very tough examination as to the whereabouts of city and suburban streets, principal buildings, hospitals, places of entertainment, docks, clubs and the quickest routes between various points.

*　*　*　*

It was in Williamson Square, however, that I got to know the men themselves a cheery humorous crowd, as they sat yarning with me by the gas-fire in the shelter.

"If I was to write a book about my experiences *Alice in Wonderland* wouldn't compare with it," Mr. Arthur Stanley Schofield, who has been 44 years a Liverpool cabby, told me. "This job is an education in itself, you meet the best and the worst."

"Pal of mine met a couple of the worst the other night," chimed in a driver at the far end of the table. "Two chaps stopped his cab and told him to drive to Cazneau Street. When they got there they refused to pay the fare and did a bunk. Old Charlie ups and out and chases them. A policeman with one of those Alsatians happened to be standing nearby and saw the whole thing. He let the dog go and it caught Charlie."

"Aye, you get some right queer customers," said the driver they called 'Have-a-Go' (cabbies, by the way, are great ones for nicknames). "A few years back there was a fellow who used to set two dogs on you as soon as you got to his house, and there was another bloke who always wanted to fight you for the fare money."

Not that there is always difficulty over getting the fare. One driver met a man off the Irish boat and drove him to an address in the suburbs. At the end of the journey the man handed the cabby a boot-box. He opened it and inside was £400 in one-pound notes. A few months later that driver met the Irish boat again and could hardly believe his eyes when he saw his previous benefactor hurrying down the gangway. Once again he drove him out to the house in the suburbs, and once again a boot-box was produced. The fare opened the box himself this time and, dividing its contents in half, handed the astonished cabby £250.

Then there was the story of the taxi cruising along Church Street when a middle-aged man signalled it, said, " Hamburg," and jumped in. " Hamburg ? " echoed the bewildered driver. " Yes, Hamburg, Germany," and off they went on what was surely the longest trip of any Liverpool taxi. The shortest, maybe, was that of a lady who hailed a cab in Lime Street at a quarter to four one afternoon and shouted, " Quick, I've got to be in Buckingham Palace by four o'clock." " Sorry, lady, I don't think I'll be able to make it by four," said the alarmed cabby, and off he drove as fast as his wheels would take him to pull himself together over a strong cup of tea in Williamson Square !

PULPITS AT PIER HEAD

JUST about the time that they are playing the last waltz at the Palais de Danse and the cinemas are emptying out untidy masses of people into the bleak Saturday-night streets, a handful of soapbox salvationists are reaching hell-fire-and-brimstone crescendos at the Pier Head.

Once upon a time it was a plot of waste land at the top of Ranelagh Street which was the chosen venue of all these perfervid pulpiteers of the street corner, but since its enclosure for building purposes there has been a migration of souls to the stony ground of the promenade above the landing-stage.

Every night you will find them there, and often in the lunch-hour too, but it is on a Saturday that the preachers are at their best, sounding their militant music of salvation loudest to usher in Sunday morning.

I went there the other Saturday and hung upon the verge of little knots of auditors beside the black glass waters of a Mersey that seemed transformed that night into a motionless Styx, beside which zealous fishers of men cast nets for returning trippers.

Alas, I did not, like Dylan Thomas, discover among their motley ranks a man who would take off his hat and set fire to his hair every now and then that he might make his message burn the brighter, but I did encounter several men whose brains seemed alight beneath the thatches of their hats, illuminated and afire with some single all-consuming idea that burned so fierce and hot within their heads that they were compelled to air it through their mouths.

There was, of course, a number of serious-minded exponents of generally-accepted religions, but it was with the cranks—the lunatic fringe of orthodox theology—that I was chiefly concerned. Cranks some of them may have been, but, however bizarre in belief, all without exception blazed with the authentic fire of absolute sincerity.

"Brother," said a fierce evangelist seizing me by the sleeve, "where do you intend to spend eternity?" I regretted my ignorance.

"And a h'angel 'overed before me with h'outspread wings and I saw the light," thundered a little man in a frayed brown suit.

"You was drunk, grandad," yelled a disrespectful voice from the crowd. "That there 'oly water 's doing for you."

The little man ignored the interruption.

"My sister's a prophetess. Hallelujah! Your shoes are getting worn. Hallelujah! Take them to the Lord. Hallelujah! I made a speech where I worked. Hallelujah! I got thrown out for it, but I wasn't worried about that. Hallelujah! That was Satan that was. Hallelujah!" I have a shrewd suspicion that it was Satan in the guise of the works manager. Hallelujah!

*   *   *   *

I moved off. A man with a bunchy umbrella suddenly opened it to reveal a whitewashed prediction of the blackest tragedy for those who heed not, and began to sing a hymn in a high cracked voice. "Swing it, mate," shouted one of the crowd.

"Give him a pint——of petrol."

And in and out between the speakers moved phalanxes of cuffed and tapered Teddy boys and their sleek but grubby girl friends, keeping up an incessant barrage of badinage and mockery. "Where was Moses when the light went out?" "Tell us about the time the devil put your bicycle wheel in the tram-lines, Dad," they jeered. They were very young and life had not yet hurt them. "He jests at scars, that never felt a wound." Somehow I could not help feeling that many of those muddled verbose Jobs, who bore imperturbably the burden of continuous insults, had known too many sores. They had been drained of something, and that something was humour.

Slowly the hands of the Liver clock crept round. One by one the little platforms were folded up and their occupants departed, each to his private hell or heaven. On the near-deserted waterfront a solitary old white-haired man stood alone in the dark crying his creed over the empty waters of the Mersey—over the waters of Lethe.

THE hoary legend of a jilted bride grieving in a house of memories where the wedding-feast mouldered to dust, and how the truth was revealed to the detriment of romance.

THE MYSTERY HOUSE OF MULGRAVE STREET

ONE of the things that always strikes me as rather a pity is that history as we know it invariably confines itself to the chronicling of great events. It is wonderfully precise regarding the dates and doings of kings and queens and windy statesmen, but turns a glory-blinded eye to the thousands of little everyday details that go to make up the background of an age. Unless it be in the published memoirs or diaries of contemporaries, or the ephemeral effusion of the journalist, these fascinating trivia have no memorial. They are forever lost or, worse, pass down by word of mouth, distorted beyond all recognition, and thus useless as history. A case in point is that of the Mystery House of Mulgrave Street whose strange story has, down the years, become part of the hitherto unwritten folklore of Liverpool.

★   ★   ★   ★

Like many another of my generation, I heard the story of the tragic bride of Mulgrave Street at my mother's knee. I listened to it spell-bound, and along with all the other nursery tales of giants and witches, of fairies good and bad, I accepted it unquestioningly. When I grew older the world soon robbed me of my childish belief in ogres, augurs and fairy-godmothers, but the legend of Mulgrave Street lingered on in the misty hinterland of my mind. It was not, in fact, until quite recently that it even occurred to me that it might possibly belong to the realm of fable.

I don't suppose I had given the old story a thought for twenty years until, lunching at my club the other day, a friend suddenly said to me, " I'm surprised you've never written-up the history of the Mystery House of Mulgrave Street." For a moment I was puzzled, and then all at once it came back to me.

At a time when I still relied upon a perambulator rather than my own two legs to convey me, peripatetic, around the streets of Liverpool, we lived in an old and rather splendid house in Upper Parliament Street. I was a somewhat delicate child and the doctor had told my parents that I should get as much fresh air as possible. On sunny afternoons I was, therefore, usually wheeled along the Boulevard to Prince's Park, but on dull days when lowering skies drooped grey with the threat of rain, my nurse would venture no farther afield with me than a hurried promenade as far as Crown Street and back. It was on those occasions, I remember, that we used to pass a dreary, three-story, red brick house whose dust-curtained windows lent to it a forlorn and distinctly sinister aspect. The house stood on the corner of Mulgrave and Upper Parliament streets, and my nurse, a super-stitious Irish girl, would always scurry past it with piously averted eyes. So far as I could discover, no one had ever been within its forbidding walls, but I gathered that it was the home of an old, old lady who had once been engaged to be married. On her wedding-morning the bride had waited at the church for the groom in vain. He never turned up, and the heartbroken girl returned alone to the house where the wedding-breakfast lay waiting. She went in, closed the door behind her and never again emerged. From that day onwards the house remained shuttered and lifeless, the table still laid, the feast turning to dust, the sorrowing bride gradually changing from a lovely young girl into an old wrinkled woman in a yellowing wedding-dress. All this I learned from my nurse, and my mother afterwards confirmed that the extraordinary tale had been current when she was a child, and added that to her certain knowledge that eerie old house had stood with its blank unlit windows and smokeless chimneys, lonely and deserted for as long as she could remember.

*   *   *   *

After that lunch-time conversation with my friend, in the course of which I discovered that he had heard, and always believed, exactly the same story as I had, I made a point of asking everyone I met if they knew anything about the house in question. Most of them did. And it was always the same thing. A jilted bride had forsaken the world to live alone in a house of memories where the wedding-breakfast crumbled to dust. The thing became an obsession and I decided that I must find out once and for all whether or not there was any truth in it.

I began by going along to the house. I found it far from lifeless. It has now been converted into flats and the voices of children have put the ghosts of the past to flight. I had a bit of difficulty in deciding whether it is really in Mulgrave Street or Upper Parliament Street, for it stretches right round the corner, and one of the tenants told me that it is regarded as both number 1 Mulgrave Street *and* number 166 Upper Parliament Street.

My next step was to make a careful search through the mouldering pages of a formidable pile of ancient Gore's Liverpool Directories. Number 166 Upper Parliament Street makes its first appearance in the street directory for the year 1880. It was then apparently a newly-erected house, and its first occupant was a Mr. Richard Holden Davis, described as an alkali manufacturer (Golding, Davis & Co.), who, prior to moving in there, had lived at number 16 Montpellier Terrace, which is just across the road. He seems to have lived at number 166 alone until 1898, when he was joined there by one Richard H. Davidson, an oil refiner of the firm of Richard Davidson & Co., of 24 Maguire Street. The following year two more gentlemen arrived, a Mr. Herbert S. Davidson and another Richard Davidson, both described as oil refiners. In 1900 all four are still in residence, but the original Richard Holden Davis is now described as ' gentleman,' by which we are presumably to understand that he has now retired from alkali manufacturing. By 1901, Joseph M. Davidson, clerk, has taken up quarters at number 166, but Richard H. Davidson has moved out to Aigburth. Throughout 1902 this *ménage à quatre* remains unchanged, but in 1903 a Miss M. R. Davis is listed as occupier of the property, and Messrs. Richard, Herbert S., and Joseph M. Davidson have all moved to Manor House, Promenade, Liscard. Miss M. R. Davis's name continues to appear in 1904, 1905 and, for the last time, in 1906, as sole tenant.

It was in March, 1906, I discovered, that, after a long illness, Richard Holden Davis died. He is buried in Smithdown Road Cemetery. From another source I learned that just before his death Mr. Davis gave the house to his maiden sister, Miss M. R. Davis, who was then about 40 years of age, and who had, no doubt, acted as his nurse.

After the death of her brother, to whom she was deeply attached, Miss Davis felt that she could not continue to live in the house which was large and full of painful memories for her. But neither could she bring herself to sell it or disturb its contents. She therefore kept it fully furnished, but closed it up and took rooms nearby. From time to time she would go in there, always alone. All the charges on the house were duly paid, and it was kept in a good state of repair. When, for instance, a chimney-stack blew down in a storm, it was rebuilt in a matter of two days. For 26 years things continued thus, and a mystified local populace, inspired maybe by memories of Dickens's Miss Havisham, invented the story of the tragic bride.

Somewhere about 1931 Miss Davis must have died—it is said that she ended her days with a nephew in Birkenhead—and in 1932 the old house reappears in Kelly's Directory. It had been bought by the Prudential Assurance Company, and from then until 1935 was occupied by three successive superintendents in the employ of that company.

Although number 166 Upper Parliament Street never again appears in the Liverpool directory after 1934, there is no reason to suppose that it underwent any further period of emptiness, and no one seeing its bright and cheerful countenance to-day would ever suspect that strange episode in its history when for more than a quarter of a century it stood silent and withdrawn, a lonely place of ghosts and a legendary abode of mystery.

*HOW, as the result of a bet, a
resourceful priest transformed the
wilderness into a Garden of Eden.*

THE SPANISH GARDEN

ALL in the blue Olympian weather it was difficult to realise that the little garden wasn't really in Spain ; that the whole thing was an elaborate and wonderfully contrived make-believe on a scarred blitzed site in the sooted heart of Liverpool.

A shrine of beauty has arisen in Catharine Street—a tiny Eden in the brick-and-mortar wilderness—at which thousands of city workers gaze enraptured as they are borne past St. Philip Neri's Church on their green bus tops.

Sitting there in *El Jardin della Nuestra Señora*—The Garden of Our Lady—I chatted to the Reverend Dr. John Garvin, the man who conceived and carried out this amazingly imaginative piece of land-scape transformation.

" It started," he told me, " as a bet. One day in 1952 I paid a visit to the Spanish roof-garden of Barker's Stores in London, and I made up my mind there and then that I would build my own Spanish garden in Liverpool. I said, somewhat rashly perhaps, that I would have my blitzed site looking like a *jardin Español* within a year."

★　　★　　★　　★

Dr. Garvin won his bet. But it was hard work transforming the brick and rubble strewn piece of waste land adjoining his church into the lush garden which burgeons there to-day, and the doctor had to take off his cassock, roll up his sleeves and get down to it in earnest.

Bit by bit, the ground was levelled off ; ton after ton of good rich soil was shovelled into place ; sunken paths were constructed and the fountains—twenty-five of them—began to play. Much ingenuity and little money had to be used. The kitchen sink of the bomb-razed house was made into a charming miniature alpine garden. Flower-tubs were knocked together out of old wine-casks and pipes of

105

port—a process accompanied by much hilarity as the fumes which clung about them were still potent enough to make it a right merry business !

Most of the architectural features—roof and wall tiles, pillars, and the Moorish battlements of the walls—were fabricated with paint-pot and cement by Dr. Garvin himself, but there were also certain importations from abroad, such as two magnificent marble columns, at least 2,000 years old, which, legend has it, came, via Lowther Castle, from the neighbourhood of the Roman Colosseum. There are, too, several local antiquities : a fragment of a pillar from Gladstone's old house in Rodney Street, and two plump cherubim which have somehow winged their stony way here from the Bluecoat School.

And to this tranquil garden have come, during the last four years, beautiful things from all over the world : quartzite from distant Italian quarries, orange-trees from white-roofed Casablanca, delicate golden faience work from Vesselay and lovely painted tiles from Spain. We paused by a white-limed wall to admire a particularly fine tile from Bilbao, brightly embellished with a representation of the *Ovación y oreja*—the matador's final address to the pic-*ed* and banderil-lad bull.

*　　*　　*　　*

Appropriately enough in a priest's garden, there is a strongly religious motif running through it all. The centre-piece is a graceful shrine to the Madonna and Child and it is flanked by two specimens of the tree of heaven. The sacred symbol seven is represented by a yucca-tree, which flowers every seven years, and a flock of seven soul-white Aylesbury ducks. Alas ! the latter have proved to be but whited sepulchres, for they have disgraced themselves by gobbling up all the carnations. For their sins, their number is being diminished as fast as the cook-pot will allow, and their place is to be taken by a columbarium of white fantails. Meanwhile, Jimmy the Mule (a kind of hybrid canary) sounds their knell on the little bell he tinkles for attention as you pass his swinging cage.

Close beside the garden well—" Some fool is bound to step into it," Dr. Garvin had said the day it was completed, and that very evening plunged knee-deep in it himself !—there is a greenhouse wherein grows a far-from-barren fig-tree, a flourish of vines and a proud cluster of passion-flowers. The priest climbed a rickety wooden ladder and, very gently, picked a single bloom. He held the little cerulean flower, which epitomises the tragic drama around which his church and his life have been built, tenderly in his hand and pointed out the instruments of Christ's Passion. They were all there : the three nails (the stigmas), the five wounds (the anthers), the crown of thorns (the red-stained rays of the corona), the scourge (a tendril tight-coiled as a watch-spring) and even the ten faithful apostles (the perianth)—Judas who betrayed and Peter who denied are missing.

It was as we were leaving this heavenly garden that I noticed the two green bay trees. " Yes," said Dr. Garvin, " they seem to like the climate of Catharine Street and flourish wickedly."

DEATH IN THE AFTERNOON

S PEKE Airport.
     Whit Monday, 21st May, 1956.
     For once the weather is idyllic.

A shimmering haze of heat blankets the bank-holiday crowd of 100,000 who have come to see the International Air Display.

The sun blazes, a blinding white-hot brazier, its brilliance stabbing off the sleek silver bodies of the planes that buzz like angry gnats through the tepid air.

The sky is Mediterranean-blue, the tarmac and terminal buildings gleam a painful Tangier-white, the grass of the airfield is scorched yellowish-brown in patches.

Children squeal with delight. Mother brings out the flask and sandwiches. Father smokes his pipe and, sprawling on the warm earth, watches the flashing aerobats through field-glasses.

The Sipa 200 Minijet zooms low. A gasp scythes across the field. The crowd involuntarily ducks—recovers to a ripple of shame-faced laughter.

On such a day it is good to be alive, but for one of the 100,000, all unsuspected, death is quietly waiting in that azure vault of sky.

Very soon now the great event of the pageant is scheduled to take place. Thousands of programmes rustle an overture of anticipation. There is a pleasant mounting of tension.

The cause of all this excitement is a slight, swarthy, 37-year-old Frenchman, Léo Valentin, who, ever since he was a small boy watching the storks and buzzards soaring above the trees of the great park that surrounded his home at Epinal in the Vosges department of France, has devoted his life to the dream of flying like a bird.

This afternoon is to see the climax of that dream for, billed as the Bird Man, he is to jump from an aircraft at 8,500 feet and, with the aid of a pair of wooden wings, attempt to glide for several miles before parachuting down onto the airfield.

Already once to-day Valentin has launched himself into space. An hour earlier he has executed a brilliant delayed parachute drop, plummeting from 8,000 feet before, just 1,000 feet above the ground, he pulled his rip-cord and with a sharp crack the billowing, white silk of his parachute blossomed out to brake his 120 m.p.h. free fall and float him at a safe 15 m.p.h. to the reassuring earth.

But *this* is his hour.

He is the last of the twentieth-century disciples of Icarus.

He is to try and realise the age-old dream of the ancient Greek, and like him he is to lose his wings.

He is to challenge the sky—and lose.

★   ★   ★   ★

Léo Valentin was born of humble parents at Epinal in 1919. Before he was ten, fascinated by aeroplanes, he was spending most of his time wandering around the hangars of Dogneville Aerodrome, gazing enraptured at the quaint flying-machines and sometimes actually talking to those leather-suited and goggled demigods, the pilots who flew them.

He left school at sixteen to become, first, a butcher's boy and then an apprentice locksmith, but the urge to fly persisted, and he scraped together sufficient money to attend lectures at the Vosges Air Club in his spare time.

In 1938, at the age of 19, he enlisted in the *Armée de l'Air*, was sent to Blida in North Africa and rapidly rose to the rank of corporal, but impatient at the prospect of the three years' pilot's course which one had to take before starting to fly, he volunteered to train as a parachutist at the Maison Blanche centre at Algiers. He made his first jump over Baraki on October 15th, 1938.

The following year war was declared and the French parachutists were for a time transformed into mountain troops, but subsequently continued their training at Montélimar.

Valentin was on the Pyrenean frontier when France fell, but he managed to escape, via the underground, to North Africa. There he joined the parachute school which had been formed at Fez and, with more than 80 jumps to his credit now, he was promptly made a sergeant-instructor.

Presently, however, the monotony of camp life began to bore him. He wanted action. And so, at the end of 1942, he embarked on a troop-transport, and a few days later found himself in Liverpool.

From there he was sent straightaway to a camp near Glasgow where the British Special Air Service was undergoing intensive training in preparation for the invasion.

On June 9th, 1944, Valentin parachuted into Brittany. He dropped over Morbihan and, after blowing up the railway lines between Vannes and Rennes, made his way to the St. Marcel Plateau.

During the next few months he took part in some fierce fighting and, after a brief respite back in England, he was sent into the Loire pocket where in the course of an engagement with the S.S. his right arm was shattered by an explosive bullet. He was treated in the hospital at Issoudun and convalesced on the Marne and in England.

At the end of the war Valentin was promoted to sergeant-major and posted as an instructor to the parachute school at Lannion. A few months later the school was transferred to Pau, and there Valentin remained until he decided to quit the *Armée de l'Air* in 1949.

It was in the Pau Library that Valentin first began to pore over certain ancient books in which was embalmed the history of man's long fight to conquer the heavens.

He read, with mounting excitement, of the pioneer parachutists, of old Fausto Veranzio, the Venetian mathematician who, in 1616, first described an apparatus resembling a parachute; of Sebastien le Normand, the father of parachuting; of Garnerin; Berry, the first parachutist to be launched from a plane; Pégoud; and the American, Irvin, who, on April 28th, 1919, jumped from an aeroplane flying at 1,800 feet and opened his parachute at 600 feet, thus accomplishing the first delayed action drop.

He read and he resolved . . . he would have *his* place in the sky.

This ambition was achieved on March 23rd, 1948, when he jumped over Pau from a height of 22,000 feet, allowing himself to fall to 1,800 feet before opening his parachute. That exploit put the world record for a free drop without a respirator in his pocket. The following November he established a new world record for a free drop without respirator by night.

During those four years at Pau Valentin made one other great advance. He invented a method of controlling his position during a free fall. After a considerable amount of perilous experimentation the Valentin position was born.

Naturally, all these activities had made Léo Valentin something of a star in the world of aviation, and when he retired from the *Armée de l'Air* he made up his mind to go in for stunt parachuting. It was now that he began to consider again the whole question of flight. He wanted to fly like a bird, and so he decided that, like a bird, he must sprout wings.

Working in secret, he made himself a pair of canvas wings. He tried them out on April 30th, 1950, at Villacoublay before a crowd of 300,000. They were not a success and nearly cost him his life. Nevertheless, he attempted a second flight with them over Meaux-Esbly Airfield on May 4th. Once again they proved unsatisfactory. Convinced by these two experiences, Valentin realised that he must abandon canvas wings. What he really needed, he told himself, were wooden feathers.

Throughout the last six months of 1950 and the first six months of 1951, Valentin and his friend Monsieur Collignon spent many, many hours in the latter's workshops on the outskirts of Paris constructing a pair of wooden wings.

Valentin made his first test jump with them at Cormeilles-en-Vexin on June 8th, 1951. He launched himself from a platform attached to the side of a helicopter. A terrific gust of wind closed the wings and he got into a terrible spin. He only just managed to pull out of it and landed with the hard-won knowledge that some way must be devised to prevent the wings from closing.

A month later, his wings now provided with automatic locks, the indomitable little Frenchman was ready to try again.

This occasion—July 2nd, 1951—was for him a rather special one, for the venue of the jump was that same Dogneville Airfield where, nearly a quarter of a century before, the young Valentin had watched and envied those heroes of the sky. He soared up to 9,000 feet in a Junkers 52 and leapt into the void. He had just time to glimpse the well-remembered landscape of his childhood spread like a tawny map below him, and then . . . he found himself plunged into a bewildering spin. The lock of his right wing had been damaged. The left wing was firm, locked, but the right hung limp and flapping at his side. The spin intensified. The earth whirled like a vortex. The blood rushed to his head. His vision blurred. On the point of fainting he just managed by a gigantic effort of will to pull the rip-cord. Trembling like a leaf, he landed on the very brink of the Moselle. It was the worst drop he had ever made.

It says much for the man's nerve that after an experience like that Valentin could ever again entrust himself to the tender mercies of those fickle wings. But victory was just around the corner. Three years later, on May 13th, 1954, at Gisy-les-Nobles, near Pont-sur-Yonne, Léo Valentin, the Bird Man, using his wooden wings, ' flew ' for a distance of at least three miles over Thorigny and landed safe and sound in a field of lucerne.

Now, two years later almost to the day, on May 21st, 1956, at Speke, Liverpool, Valentin is to experiment with a new pair of wings. They are of bright orange-coloured balsa-wood. Four feet high, and with an overall span of 9 feet, they are attached to a light metal alloy corset and fitted with ailerons. The whole apparatus weighs 28 lb.

The Bird Man is to fly again and I am to fly with him.

*   *   *   *

It is 3-40 p.m. precisely.

I follow the diminutive figure of the Bird Man across the tarmac

111

and clamber after him into the waiting Dakota.

Five minutes later the engines are revving up.

We begin to taxi slowly out to the runway.

" Un moment ! Un moment ! " shouts Valentin.

He has forgotten something.

He leaps out, runs across the tarmac to a small shed.

A minute or so later he is back with a box spanner.

He makes a last-minute adjustment to his left wing.

We move off again.

At 3-55 we roar along the field. The ground drops away.

We are airborne.

We bank out over the River Mersey, describe a vast circle over Cheshire, climb steadily to 9,000 feet. The earth is spread out below us like a green patchwork quilt. It looks far away.   Very harmless. The late afternoon sun glints gold across great cotton-woolly patches of cumulus cloud bunched like irregular icebergs in a blue and misty sea of sky.

It is cold in the plane. Icy air comes rushing in through the 7-foot gap where the port-side freight doors have been removed to facilitate the Bird Man's exit.

I glance at Valentin. He is sitting hunched like a broody bird on the back seat. The wind ruffles his hair, combed straight back over his balding head. It stands up like the crest of a bird. He seems nervous—ill at ease. He crouches on the very edge of the seat. Sucks his lips. Keeps looking out of the window. Oddly enough, he confesses that he hates heights. An ascent of the Eiffel Tower once made him sick.

4-06. We top 9,000 feet and then drop to 8,500, the height from which the jump is to be made.

" Five minutes from now," says the pilot.

Valentin rises to his feet. Struggles into his parachutes. He fixes his main parachute to his back.

" Four minutes."

He straps another to his chest. That is his emergency 'chute. On top of it is a wooden panel carrying a stop-watch and an altimeter.

" Three minutes."

Tension increases in the plane. I find myself noticing little things. The bright blue wool jumper he wears under his olive-green flying-suit, the brown lamb's-wool-lined, suède boots with zip-fasteners and crêpe soles to take the shock on landing, the large gold ring on the little finger of his left hand. I notice, too, his watch. I am to see it again on his wrist. He will be dead, but that watch will still be going.

" Two minutes."

He puts on his goggles and crash helmet and a pair of red rubber gloves, rough-surfaced like those used by a gardener or wicket-keeper.

With his hands he indicates that his heart is fluttering.

He crouches down in front of the wings and starts to adjust the straps.

" One minute."

Valentin is nowhere near ready.

4-11. " Now ! "

" Non. Non. Non ! " says Valentin.

We begin a second circuit.

" Five minutes from now," says the pilot.

The Bird Man steps into his wings. He is facing the back of the aircraft.

" Four minutes."

He gazes wistfully out of the open hatch. The ground below looks like an unreal map.

" Three minutes."

" Is the plane with the photographers alongside ? " asks Valentin.

" Two minutes."

Squatting on his heels, he edges, infinitely slowly, forward to the hatch.

" One minute."

4-16. We reach the jumping point for the second time.

" Now ! "

Valentin leans outwards.

" Non. Non. Non ! " he almost screams. " À gauche. À gauche. À gauche. La rivière à gauche." He wants the Mersey on the left.

I find this hesitation strange. It seems to me almost as if Valentin has a premonition. I *know* he does not want to jump. Maybe some little voice deep inside him whispers that below is death through a mist of cloud.

For the third time we start that circuit.

Again Valentin asks : " The other plane, is it alongside ? "

" Five minutes from now," says the pilot.

Once more Valentin begins to edge towards the hatch. He fights the roaring blustering gale that plucks at his clumsy wings.

" Four minutes."

Inch by inch, he advances.

" Three minutes."

His wing-tips keep catching in the ridging of the metal floor.

" Two minutes."

There can be no mistaking the strain he is undergoing. He shuffles doggedly forward into the main aperture.

" One minute."

I go over to Valentin, pat him on the shoulder and say " Bonne chance."

He pulls a wry face, gives the thumbs up signal and replies, " Merci, monsieur."

4-21. " Now ! "

What happens now happens so quickly that it is difficult to be sure of it.

Valentin steps backwards and sideways to the brink of the exit, his closed wings held straight in front of him, his body bent, leaning backwards and half supported by the outside pressure. He looks rapidly up, once, . . . down, twice, and then it seems to me a buffet of wind catches him and whips him out of the aircraft into the slipstream. At the same time I hear a terrible splintering noise above the roar of the engines. I see a tiny fragment of orange wood whisked away by the wind. Another piece hits the fuselage and goes spiralling like an autumn leaf to earth. The Bird Man has clipped his left wing on the side of the exit hatch.

A second, less than a second, later there is another crack, and the plane, which has been flying so smoothly that you could have balanced a threepenny bit in it, gives a slight rock. For a moment I am afraid that our tailplane may have been fatally damaged. All is well, however, but Valentin is in serious trouble.

Leaning out, I am almost caught in the slipstream myself, but I catch a glimpse of him. He is spinning, clock-wise, towards the earth like a top—rolling, spiralling, madly pirouetting to certain death—his smashed orange wings glistening in the sunlight.

He has two chances—two parachutes.

We bank off to the left.

Anxiously circle above his tumbling body.

Watch helplessly.

He has fallen, I should judge, about 1,000 feet, when I see a little puff of white.

His parachute is opening.

But no. Instead of mushrooming out it remains cylindrical like a candle—a Roman candle—the stuck silk rippling like a flame.

Chance number one is lost.

Down . . . down . . . down, although he is plummeting at 120 m.p.h. the fall seems interminable. Time is eternity up here. To Valentin it must seem a lifetime.

What about that second parachute on his chest ?

Heart-in-mouth, I strain to see.

He is about 1,000 feet from the ground.

IT OPENS.

It fails to develop.

God ! *that* has candled, too. It lashes around his face and wraps itself about his body like a shroud. I see him frantically struggling to free himself . . .

The long agony is almost over now.

The plane dives steeply in the wake of Valentin to within a few score feet of the ground.

And there below me in a green-and-yellow cornfield, spread-eagled, I see the figure of a bird—a bird with splayed and broken wings. He lies on his face, absolutely still, the only movement a slight ruffling of the white silk that looks from this height for all the world like the snowy pinions of a swan.

L'Homme-Oiseau a perdu ses ailes.

*   *   *   *

In his autobiography, *Bird Man*,* Léo Valentin wrote : " While I am falling the idea of death never enters my head . . . Death is for the others, not for you," and he would often say : " I always get the firm conviction before I do anything that I am going to come out alive."

And had not his optimism been justified ?

After all, it was eighteen years since he first discovered " that dark mistress, fear " in the sky above Baraki.

" The laws of gravity are inescapable and ruthlessly punish anyone who is ignorant of them or tries to flout them." But had he not dived more than 600 times into the spacious jaws of death ? And was he not still alive ?

Now, as he landed at Dover on this sunny Friday—May 18th, 1956—and drove his 12 h.p. Peugot car up through the lovely, blossom-washed English countryside to Liverpool, he thought how lucky he had been. He remembered all those others who had ' made a dent in the ground '—young Raoul Sabé, his army comrade whom he had seen plunge to his death on October 13th, 1938, just two days before he had to make his own first drop ; Clem Sohn, that *other* bird man, Salvator Canarrozzo, and that sweet girl, Baby Monetti.

It was a warm day, but he shuddered.

" I am nearly forty," he told himself. " It is well that this madness should stop. You cannot continue to stretch the limits of what is possible without provoking death—and that slut is not very loving if you flout her or pretend to ignore her."

Yes, this would definitely be his last jump.

He would receive £200 for it. That was the sum he needed to complete the deposit on the little provincial cinema which he was going to buy to support him in his retirement.

This time nothing must go wrong.

He booked a single room at the Airport Hotel at Speke. He asked for room 123—that would be lucky because it was the signal he counted before baling out.

Valentin spent the next couple of days in preparation.

His wings were kept in a locked room at the airport. He guarded them closely and allowed no one but himself to touch them.

* *Published in English translation by Messrs. Hutchinson in 1955.*

The Dakota from which he was to make his jump had been hired from the Liverpool air charter company, Starways Ltd., and flown specially from the south of France for the occasion.

On the Sunday Valentin inspected it and expressed himself dissatisfied with the door from which he was to make his exit. He thought it too narrow. " If I have to jump through the ordinary door," he said, " the slipstream will catch my wings before I am properly out and wedge me in the door."

He insisted that the freight doors would have to be removed.

This meant getting Ministry permission.

It was granted and, after ordering that both sides of the emergency hatch should be padded for fear he damaged his wings on them, Valentin signed a declaration certifying his satisfaction with the aircraft.

Just what it was that went wrong the next day we shall never know.

Looking down at his rapidly-receding figure, I could not begin to guess.

Looking up, a hundred thousand people far below were none the wiser.

They saw the silver Dakota circle the airport twice before a tiny object appeared, dropping like a stone.

They waited for the start of the bird-like flight.

Nothing happened.

They listened for the commentary.

The loud-speakers were silent.

An observer on the ground, watching through powerful binoculars, said afterwards : " I saw the Bird Man leave the plane quite clearly. He seemed to jump awkwardly at first, but levelled out and everything seemed all right. There was no suggestion of a glide, however, and when he had fallen about 1,000 feet I saw a canopy and lines streaming out from him. Then his parachute candled and I could make him out frantically struggling to release his harness and level up. A little later I saw a billow of white silk. It was his second parachute. Then he disappeared behind a hangar and I knew that it had opened too late. The Bird Man had done his last act."

Another man, who saw Valentin hurtle over the rooftops of a housing estate and across a lane and railway line, lived on the edge of the field at Yew Tree Farm, Higher Road, Halewood, into which he crashed. He told me : " As I saw him plunging towards the ground at a terrific speed I heard a noise like the crying of a flock of seagulls— it was the Bird Man screaming."

As soon as we in the plane saw that Valentin was in trouble, the pilot radioed for help to Speke. The message was relayed by airport control to Lieutenant-Commander L. Tivy, a Fleet Air Arm pilot who had been patrolling the Mersey in a helicopter in case Valentin dropped into the river. We transmitted the fallen Bird Man's exact position and saw the helicopter speeding like a grey gnat to the rescue.

Meanwhile, the first to reach Valentin was a Mr. George D. Hoyland of Formby. He had been driving along Higher Road when he first caught sight of Valentin. " He was at about 1,500 feet and I could see he was in trouble. His parachute didn't open and he went into a dizzy spin, crashing to the ground. I got out of the car and ran across the field to him."

The naval helicopter arrived. Landed. Then it rose again to chase an ambulance which was heading in the wrong direction.

A doctor came on the scene. He had covered the two miles from the airfield in record time. Strangely enough, although I did not know it at the time, it was my own doctor—Dr. Mesrovb Barseghian.

Police-Constable Sevill of the Lancashire County Police, also summoned by radio to the spot, removed the parachute from Valentin's back to facilitate medical examination.

Dr. Barseghian bent over him.

He made a quick examination.

Severe head injuries. Broken legs.

There would have been no pain.

Death was instantaneous.

They covered him with his parachute—it was his shroud.

* * * *

At midday on Friday, May 25th, 1956, just one week to the day after he had landed so cheerfully at Dover, we sat in the pink and eau-de-nil coroner's court-room at Widnes Police Station to hold an inquest on Léo Valentin.

For nearly an hour a procession of those of us who had in one way or another shared his last hours filed into the box to tell Mr. Cornelius Bolton, the South-West Lancashire Coroner, what we knew.

Mr. Charles Forbes Sealey, a retired group-captain employed by the Soldiers, Sailors and Air Force Association (on whose behalf the Speke Air Display had been organised) gave evidence of identification.

Mr. James Murray Kent, traffic manager of Starways Ltd., who had acted as liaison officer in the Dakota, told of Valentin's last moments in the plane. He said that on landing he examined the aircraft but found no indication that the Bird Man had struck the wings or tailplane unit.

Mr. Edwin Robert James, an aircraft fitter employed by Starways Ltd., said that when, later, he unrolled the carpet in the plane he found a piece of orange-coloured balsa-wood, about six inches long, which he realised was part of the wings used by Valentin.

Captain George Leigh, pilot of the aircraft, testified that before the ascent he had had some conversation with Valentin. He had told him that he had war-time experience of dropping parachutists and offered to 'feather' the port engine if the Bird Man thought there was any risk of his being sucked out, but Valentin replied, "No, it's not necessary." Captain Leigh said that he was flying at 105 knots (120 m.p.h.) when Valentin jumped, and added that at that speed the tailplane was well out of the way. "I am certain that he did not hit the tail. A man of Valentin's weight hitting the tailplane would certainly have knocked it off. Even a sea-gull striking the aircraft at that speed would have dented it. There would have been a considerable disturbance to the aircraft if Valentin had gone even within ten feet of the tail." He concluded by saying that he, too, had dropped from a Dakota, and was convinced that the fact that Valentin clipped his wings on his way out of the plane was purely incidental. In his opinion, the Bird Man had made a bad exit and that was what caused him to spin.

Two of Valentin's compatriots also gave evidence.

The first, Inspector Jean Albert Errard of the French police, said that he was a friend of Valentin's and happened to be in England on holiday from Paris when he read of his death in the newspapers. "I knew him very well when I served with him as a parachutist in the British Special Air Service from 1943 to the end of the war. He lived at Brunoy and has given many exhibitions of parachute jumping in France." He gave formal evidence of identification. Inspector Errard confided to me that it was his personal opinion that Valentin must have blacked out when he jumped. "He was too experienced a parachutist to make such a mistake," he said.

The second, Monsieur René Chancerel, Principal of the Biscarrosse State Parachute School, near Biarritz, said that he had made 190 jumps himself, four or five of them from Dakotas. He had examined the two parachutes after the fall and his expert testimony brought a little light into dark places. M. Chancerel explained that Valentin apparently caught the edge of his left wing on the corner of the hatchway. He immediately fell into a spin and pulled the ripcord of the parachute on his back at about 6,900 feet. The spin was so rapid, however, that the rigging lines became completely entangled. Indeed, they were later seen to have become plaited into a single thick rope. He used his chest parachute too late, as evidenced by the fact that part of the cordage remained in the container. M. Chancerel agreed with Captain Leigh that the clipping of the wings as Valentin exited was a matter of little moment, and that the main cause of the accident was a bad exit that developed the spin.

Dr. Mesrovb Barseghian then went into the box. He said that he was on duty at a first-aid post at the airfield and went in response to a broadcast message to the spot where Valentin had fallen. The

Bird Man had apparently landed on his knees. His face was smashed and bleeding and he was extensively cyanosed. There had been no post-mortem, but he had no hesitation in ascribing Valentin's death to multiple injuries of the head.

On the coroner's direction the jury returned a verdict of " Death by Misadventure."

" There is no doubt," said Mr. Bolton, " that Monsieur Valentin met his death as the result of an accident. There is no question of the aircraft not having been flown in a proper way."

He then told a hushed court-room :

" This is a very sad case. This man, apparently very air-minded, a pioneer in his own sphere, lost his life like many pioneers in the world of aviation. We are very sorry indeed that he lost his life in such an unfortunate manner."

It was a pity that there was no relative of Valentin's there to hear that tribute. He had been married once and had a 13-year-old daughter, but he and his wife had drifted apart. As it was, Monsieur A. Pierre, the French Vice-Consul in Liverpool, who was present, rose and thanked the court for its sympathy. He bowed. We trickled out into the sunlight. An aeroplane purred overhead.

★　★　★　★

When I left the coroner's court I decided to say my last farewell to the gallant little Valentin.

His body was in the mortuary at Whiston Hospital while arrangements were being made for it to be flown back to France in a French military plane the following Tuesday.

Four days ago, at the time of the tragedy, there had seemed something almost grand about it. It was drama of the highest order. Grandiloquent phrases about the blood of Icarus and those who flew in his wake not having spattered the earth in vain sprang to one's mind. Now, seeing him lying so quietly there, the whole thing suddenly struck me as terribly pathetic—the little man who hated heights journeying alone, friendless, to a foreign country, speaking not a word of its language, to die among strangers, smashed to pieces on alien soil.

Thank God, death would, as Dr. Barseghian had said, have been instantaneous.

★　★　★　★

Driving back to Liverpool I had to pass close to the spot where the Bird Man fell. I had only seen it from the air. On an impulse, I stopped the car, crossed into the field of corn. Yes, there they were, two dark depressions in·the green earth—that was where his knees

119

and chin had struck the ground. But what were all those little bunches of flowers ? A farm labourer told me. They were tributes of lilac, blue irises and *muguets des bois* scattered to his memory by local children.

It was a heavenly day.

Larks sang.

I gazed up at the sky.

It was blue—like a baby's eyes.

How innocent it looked.

But then, why shouldn't it ?

It was the earth that killed Léo Valentin for, as he himself once wrote :

" The lost parachutist knows the face of death. It is the face of the earth."

*A STREET index including
Index Street and Every Street
in Liverpool, though X Street is
conspicuous by its absence.*

THE CALL OF THE ROAD

FRANKLY, I have never counted them, but I am assured by those who ought to know that there are something like 5,000 streets in Liverpool, which, end to end, total up to a distance of more than 723 miles. Whichever way you look at it, that's an awful lot of streets, and it occurs to me that the business of finding names for them all must have occasioned quite a few headaches for quite a number of people.

From A (Alpha Street) to Z (Zante Street) every letter of the alphabet has its neat little contingent of names below it in the Liverpool street directory—every letter except X. Will not some bold spirit among the street-naming fraternity make his mark by adding an X to the list ? I suggest Xanthian (pertaining to Xanthus an ancient town in Asia Minor), Xantippe (the wife of Socrates), Xeres (an Andalusian town which is justly commemorated in ' sherry '), or, should the street be sword-shaped, it could most aptly be designated Xiphoid.

Sometimes invention seems to have been so sorely taxed that it has proved necessary to take a leaf out of the London street guide, for Liverpool boasts a Paddington, a Strand, a Kensington, a Whitechapel, a Pall Mall, a Covent Garden, and an Islington. It has also an Oxford Street, a Waterloo Road, Harley and Wimpole streets, a Fleet Street, a Downing Street, a Soho Street and even a Regent Street. Only for Piccadilly must one take a train to Manchester. But if Liverpool has borrowed from London, then surely the capital is also indebted to us, for it possesses seven Liverpool Roads, one Liverpool Street and a Liverpool Grove, not to mention an Allerton Road, a Lime Street, a Dale Street, a Lord Street, a Paradise Street and a Mersey Road.

*   *   *   *

The most casual glance through a street index will show you that Liverpool has plundered pretty well every department of life for its street names. The English towns and counties are well represented—Arundel, Bristol, Bedford, Cumberland, Devonshire, Essex, Gloucester, Leeds, Malvern, Salisbury, Worcester and York. From further afield come Abyssinia and Ethiopia streets, California and Pennsylvania roads, Egypt, Cairo and Nile streets, Roman Street, Russian Avenue and Moscow and Kremlin drives. Art contributes Gainsborough and Hogarth roads, and Vandyke, Rembrandt and Rubens streets. Music gives us Verdi, Handel, Mozart, Schubert and Rossini streets, and Haydn and Elgar roads. From literature come Chaucer, Shakespeare, Alexander Pope, Hemans, Dickens, Brontë, Thackeray, Wilde and Whitman streets. Great statesmen—Gladstone, Pitt, Beaconsfield, Garibaldi and Roosevelt; religious leaders—Wesley, Wycliffe, Luther and Spurgeon; scientists—Newton, Dalton, Faraday, Kelvin and Huxley; eminent soldiers and sailors—Wellington, Kitchener, Nelson, Grenville and Collingwood, are all commemorated.

Sometimes you can almost hear the minds of the christeners creaking with the strain. To what *ultima Thule* of agonised brain-rackings must they have been driven before they decided, one suspects with a shrug, on Borax Street, Hygeia Street and Phythian and Pluto streets. "We really can't have another Victoria Street, there are 9 Liverpool thoroughfares named after her already," they would say tugging pensively at their beards, "and there are 6 Kings, 9 Queens, 14 Princes, 21 Churches, 11 Chapels, 6 Oxfords and 5 Cambridges." Maybe it was after some such abortive session as this that Dam Lane was named! Indeed, so phrenetic did they become about the whole business that they were guilty of one or two pieces of gross carelessness. There is, for instance, a Netherfield Road North and a Netherfield Road South, but there is no Netherfield Road in Liverpool. Similarly, there is, as an astute murderer was once quick to appreciate, a Menlove Gardens North, a Menlove Gardens South and a Menlove Gardens West, but Menlove Gardens East does not exist.

★　　★　　★　　★

Some of the names that *were* bestowed on streets were . . . lamentable. What a fool you would feel if when asked in what street you lived you had to reply " Ono Street." Nanoose Road and Nebo Street strike me as equally unfortunate, while Boycott Street sounds positively unsociable. Then there are others that tempt one to facetiousness. Is it always cold in Arctic Road, freezing in Frost Street and correspondingly warm in Coal Street? Are they all madly gay in Cheers Street? Does everybody embrace the bottle in Zig Zag Road? Are there any turnings in Long Lane? Are the residents in

Crooked Lane and Askew Street absolutely straight ? Do they know all the answers in Index Street ? If they do, maybe they can tell me something about Hadassah Grove. I chanced upon it the other day, a quiet green backwater near the singing highways of Lark and Linnet lanes. The moment I saw that unexpected name on its neat white plaque it struck me as being as oddly out of context as a solitary Indian among a company of Eskimos. I don't know why it evoked the feeling of India—the nearest approach to the name that I have been able to find is Hadashah and that is in Palestine—but as I stood gazing down its narrow poplar-guarded length I found myself remembering, for no reason in particular, Pondicherry Lodge, which, as you will no doubt recall, was the Norwood residence of Major Sholto, late of the Indian Army, to which, somewhere about the year 1888, Mr. Sherlock Holmes was summoned to a slight case of murder. I felt that the houses in Hadassah Grove would prove to be so many Pondicherry Lodges. Inside them would be stools made of elephants' feet, huge gongs, tiger-skin rugs and lots of those little Benares brass ware tables. In their gardens I should find bells from distant temples. Upturned, their brazen tongues plucked out, they would be filled with flowers and stand in the place of Grecian urns. I might even glimpse the spare sun-dried figure of an Indian colonel tossing back a sundown chota peg.

But no, it was not a bit like that. It was all utterly English. The houses were old and comfortable-looking. In the ornate tracery of fanlights and embellishment of knockers, was reflected the solid assurance of Victorian builders. I looked in vain for a shade of the sinister. A young mother weeded her garden. Her baby slept peacefully in its pram. The only symbol of the Mysterious East was a large tiger-striped cat dosing in the late afternoon sun. But the mystery of how Hadassah Grove got its name remains. Not all the resources of the Picton Library could solve that one. The city archivist was apologetic, but it is thanks to him that I can now boast that I know the location of Every Street in Liverpool—it is off West Derby Road.

THE dust-sheets are reverently lifted from the bric-a-brac of scores of broken lives, and a septuagenarian lady plays with her childhood dolls.

TREASURE, TRAGEDY AND TRIVIA IN STORE

IN these last days I have been lifting the dust-sheets that shroud a thousand dreams which crowd the chill acres of Liverpool's huge furniture storehouses.

Perhaps at a first glance such places look, with their vast tangled forests of furniture, rather like gigantic auction-rooms, but there is a subtle difference in atmosphere, for whereas the sale-room represents the end of a dream, the depository usually signifies only a temporary eclipse.

Usually, but not always.

Back in 1878 a young Liverpool girl got married. Prior to the wedding the couple had furnished a cosy little home for themselves, but tragedy struck before they were able to move into it. The husband died on his honeymoon. The grief-stricken wife immediately telegraphed to a Liverpool depository : " I cannot bear to look upon our furniture. It holds too many memories for me. Please take it away and store it." Nor did she ever see it again. For fifty years it lay, a ghostly pyramid, in the warehouse, until at last the bride, by then an old and withered woman, died, and it was sold.

" Is this a record ? " I was tempted to ask. Not quite. That marathon storage was just beaten by a young medical student who, in 1900, deposited a trunk of medical books in a Liverpool warehouse. For more than half a century that trunk has never been opened, but every year the storage fee has been duly paid, and in 1955 a bent old man of seventy-seven called to pay the dues on his now valueless books.

*　　*　　*　　*

And that is the amazing thing about the storage business. A good fifty per cent. of the objects which are stored are of little or no intrinsic worth. They are to be evaluated only in terms of sentiment.

"Now take the case of the old lady who brought along two large cases which she said held her most prized possessions," said the warehouse-man. "They proved to contain a large assortment of her childhood dolls, and twice a year, regular as clockwork, she would come to the warehouse and spend a couple of hours playing with them ! It was really uncanny to see the slight, child-like figure with the wrinkled face kneeling there in the twilight crooning over those mouldering dolls." Shades of Miss Havisham !

Almost every depository has its trunks of faded love-letters, but one warehouseman told me of an extraordinary chest, left there twenty-four years ago by an elderly gentleman, in which are neat piles of centuries-old silk, satin, brocade, lace and frill worn by one of his ancestors.

Possibly one of the most curious objects at present lodged in any Liverpool warehouse is a spear. This spear belongs to a gentle-man who lives abroad, and once in the long-ago that very spear was thrown at him. A native servant pulled it out and, fortunately, the aforesaid gentleman suffered no injury more permanent than a hole in his back which, he claims, fits exactly the head of the spear. Every two years he comes on holiday to England and the depository always receives a postcard saying : " Please get my goods out." Shortly afterwards he himself arrives, the spear (which he always insists must be kept carefully wrapped up—" It is tipped with deadly poison ") is produced, he gazes at it for a few minutes and that is that for another couple of years.

Another regular visitor is a man who first put in an appearance a number of years ago. He came upon the scene wearing a heavy fur overcoat, and brought with him a single large trunk which he said contained his summer clothes. The following spring he reappeared, asked for his trunk and requested permission to change his clothes. He did so and deposited his fur coat and woolly winter underwear in the trunk. And every spring and autumn since, this curious man has called to change his clothes.

*　　*　　*　　*

From time to time among the sober piles of furniture, the rolls of carpet, the wardrobes, the dining-room suites, the broken-down mangles and the curiously pathetic little heaps of children's toys, you will find some very strange objects. The cask containing Uncle Alfred ; a captain's uniform which saw service in the Crimean War ; a penny-farthing bicycle ; a skeleton in a black, coffin-like box from a doctor's home ; bulky packages of Russian bank-notes (now worth-less) stored by a fleeing Russian aristocrat at the time of the revolution; African idols ; stuffed pets ; the grinning head of an Egyptian mummy which was said to have come out of Pharaoh's tomb. This latter, by the way, was left unclaimed for many years and eventually the proprietor took it to his own home, but his wife said that she would not sleep with the thing in the house and it finished up as a somewhat macabre exhibit in a prominent Liverpool dentist's surgery. Once, an entire farm—excluding livestock—was put into storage and, many years ago, an old Liverpool depository stored all the animals in the menagerie of Hengler's Circus. " Feeding the lions," I was told, " was quite a problem."

But the strangest story of all is that of the day when a bronzed colonial drove up in a taxi, to the front of which was lashed a huge barrel. " Say, can I store this barrel for two or three months with you ? " he asked. The manager eyed the sinister-looking barrel somewhat uneasily. " I must ask you what it contains," he said. " Opals," was the reply. And sure enough that barrel was crammed with thousands of pounds worth of precious stones. Too large to go through the door of the strong-room, the barrel was hidden beneath a pile of rubbish in the yard at the back of the depository. And there it remained until, three months later, the owner turned up with another taxi to remove his precious barrel and a great weight from the mind of the warehouseman !

A STRANGE EPISODE IN THE HISTORY OF A CHURCH

TWENTY or so feet up on the red brick face of an unobtrusive
church on the darker side of Upper Parliament Street, there is a
largish arched recess. Empty now, it looks as if it should contain
a statue, and once upon a time it did—that of a woman with a babe
in her arms.

In a way, the disappearance of that statue was closely linked
with certain dark events which took place thirty-four years before—
a strange episode in the history of a church which led to the violent
deaths of two men and a woman.

★   ★   ★   ★

The story begins on the first day of the year 1883, when there
was opened in Falkland Street, off Islington, a new church designated
the Church of Humanity and dedicated to a somewhat novel religion
known as Logical Positivism.

This religion was based on the materialistic philosophy of Auguste
Comte, a curious man who, having failed in an attempt to drown himself in the Seine and wearied John Stuart Mill and Sir William
Molesworth with his clamant and persistent demands for money,
succumbed to cancer in 1857.

In some respects the Positivist creed approximated to the Nietz-
schean concept of superman, but, less aristocratic, it dethroned the gods
of current belief and set up the welfare of mankind as object of worship
in their place. Discounting the first stage of the human mind (religious
beliefs), ignoring the second (metaphysical ideals), it concentrated its
attentions upon what it regarded as the third and highest stage (the
positivist), and sought, by means of a reassessment of social and moral
values in the light of the exact sciences, to reconstruct the fabric of
society and foster a perfect social harmony. Just how it proposed to

do this seems a little vague, but outside the Falkland Street church was blazoned the invincible trinity of Positivist dicta :

" Love for Principle
Order for Basis
Progress for Aim."

The evangel in Liverpool owed its beginnings to a Dr. Richard Carson and a Mr. Albert Crompton, the son of Judge Crompton and a prominent member of a big Liverpool shipping firm. On the death of Carson, the apostolate devolved upon Albert Crompton who held office until his death in Paris in 1904. He was succeeded by Mr. Sydney Style, a Liverpool solicitor, who lived at number 69 Hope Street.

Bald, acquiline and bearded, Mr. Style fulfilled the position of leader of the sect with distinction, not only presiding at the Sunday evening devotional meetings at Falkland Street, but also throwing his own home open for social soirées every Thursday night.

By 1913, thirty years after its foundation, the Positivist Society, its members now about 150 strong, was quietly flourishing. Many of the congregation were people of substance, and work was almost complete on a fine new church which had been built, close to Mr. Style's home, on the Upper Parliament Street corner of Hope Street. Embellished with a large statue of the Society's symbolic mother and child, it was to replace the old church in Falkland Street, and was to be known as the Temple of Humanity. During the three decades of their existence, the Positivists might not have made any spectacular contribution to the welfare of mankind in Liverpool, but at least they had done no harm, and one cannot but feel that fate was needlessly cruel when, towards the end of that year, it dealt to that innocent company of eccentrics a blow from which it was never really to recover.

★   ★   ★   ★

It was in the unlikely person of an illiterate, 23-year-old journeyman-joiner, William M'Donald, that the unsuspecting Positivists met their downfall.

M'Donald, whose family lived in Rishton Street, Everton, was an almost fanatic adherent of dialectical materialism. A keen socialist in the militant tradition of Shaw, Wells and Mr. Keir Hardie, it was only to be expected that he would subscribe wholeheartedly to any philosophy that preached the establishment of socialism on a scientific basis as a religion. Although never a member of the Positivist congregation, M'Donald had, since he was eighteen, attended educational evening-classes organised by the Church of Humanity, and was a frequent visitor at Mr. and Mrs. Style's Thursday evening soirées. A shabby undistinguished figure, whose wisp of beard betrayed the

128

fact that he had never shaved, M'Donald seemed curiously out of place in the big L-shaped room with its tinkling grand-piano and liberal buffet. He moved freely among the guests, the perpetual, self-complacent smile on his lips belying the real unease of his heart, but always his restless eyes searched for Miss Crompton.

Mary Crompton, a 42-year-old spinster, was the daughter of that Albert Crompton who had preceded Mr. Style as Positivist prophet-in-chief. She was, in consequence, an important member of the Society, and she had shown many, quite impersonal, little kindnesses to the gauche M'Donald. She seems, indeed, to have been an exceptionally kindly woman, for at least two other members of that small circle had reason to be grateful to her goodness of heart.

One of these was a young man named Richard Price Roberts. He was by trade a copper engraver and he was a member of the Church of Humanity. Actually, it was he who first introduced M'Donald to the Positivists, having made his acquaintance at a socialist meeting near St. George's Hall.

The other was 24-year-old Paul Gaze who, having been left an orphan at an early age, was adopted (though not legally) by Miss Crompton, who made herself responsible for his education, welfare and upbringing. As he grew older, Gaze formed an ardent attachment for his benefactress. She, bewildered and somewhat overcome by it all, did everything in her power to discourage his attentions, and eventually he went as the representative of a London chemical-manufacturing firm to Brazil. There, he met and fell in love with a young Brazilian girl and, much relieved, Miss Crompton, who was an accomplished linguist and spoke Portuguese fluently, went to Brazil and brought the young couple back to Liverpool to be married.

William M'Donald, Richard Price Roberts, Paul Gaze and Mary Crompton—those are the *dramatis personae*.

Sydney Style's hospitable home in Hope Street and the rising edifice of the Temple of Humanity—that is the back-cloth.

The stage is set.

The actors are assembled.

Now is the time for the curtain-rise—and fall.

*   *   *   *

Shortly after 9-30 p.m. on the evening of Tuesday, October 7th, 1913, William M'Donald rang the bell at 142 Islington, the house where Richard Price Roberts lodged. In his pocket was a fully-charged, five-chambered revolver, several loose cartridges and a razor. In his hand, a stout, foot-long cane, tipped with a heavy iron knob. When Roberts opened the door, M'Donald dealt him a vicious blow on the head with the cane, drew forth the revolver and fired two shots at him. Somewhat stunned, but otherwise uninjured, the terrified Roberts made a bolt for his bedroom. M'Donald made no attempt to follow him, but ran off into the night.

From there M'Donald made his way to Grove Street where he met Paul Gaze. He accompanied him to his lodgings at number 62. The pair went into the front room together. At about 10-15 p.m. the servant-girl, Elizabeth Taylor, heard two revolver shots, followed by the sounds of M'Donald's hurried departure. Trembling, she pushed open the parlour door. Gaze was lying in the fireplace. He was quite dead. He had been shot through the temple. A second bullet was lodged in his arm.

Meanwhile, M'Donald was knocking at the door of number 81 Bedford Street South—Miss Crompton's home. Miss Crompton had retired upstairs, but M'Donald told the maid that he wanted to see her on a matter of the utmost urgency. " I suppose I must go down," said Miss Crompton wearily to Miss Huckwell, who had been her companion for twenty-seven years. M'Donald was waiting in the sitting-room. As soon as Miss Crompton entered he shot her through the temple. Then he turned the gun on himself.

Detectives found Miss Crompton lying on the sitting-room floor. Directly opposite her, also on the floor, was M'Donald. He, too, had a bullet wound in his temple, but he was not dead. He was rushed to the Royal Infirmary, but he died at 2-30 the following morning without recovering consciousness.

*　　*　　*　　*

Oddly enough, it is to the first tenet of Positivism that we must turn for an explanation of that long-ago night of tragedy—" Love for Principle."

Poor, half-educated William M'Donald had fallen violently in love with Miss Crompton. In the words of one who knew her, " It was impossible to imagine anyone less like *une femme fatale* than she was, but that was the part she was called upon to play at the fall of the curtain. A lady of uncertain age, she was in no way beautiful— just faded and very weary. Her clothes were undeniably expensive, but lacked chic. The wonder of it is that this marcescent spinster, who looked older than her years, should have inspired passion in the breasts of two youths "—one of whom cared so much that he killed her.

All the evidence clearly establishes that there was nothing whatsoever between Miss Crompton and M'Donald. They met alone only once—on the night of her death. True, on one occasion she did call at his home—he was ill and she came to make kindly inquiries of his family. Indeed, it was probably because she seemed unmoved by his attentions that M'Donald shot her, and there is no doubt that he murdered the unfortunate Gaze in a fit of jealousy because of his resentment of his relationship with her. Roberts, too, was closely associated with Miss Crompton, and for no other reason M'Donald attempted to kill him.

The circumstances of Gaze's death were particularly tragic, for he had just returned with his Brazilian bride from his honeymoon. It was a strict rule of the Positivist creed that newly-married couples should sleep apart and meet only for meals during the first three months of their marriage. Gaze was killed before those three months had elapsed so the marriage was never consummated.

The Church of Humanity never really recovered from the effects of this terrible scandal, although it struggled on for another quarter of a century.

Mr. and Mrs. Style could still be seen walking, rather forlornly, from their house to the nearby Temple. On Sunday 8 Shakespeare 74 (16th September, 1928), they celebrated their golden wedding there, and the Sacrament of Presentation was conferred upon their grandson, David Sydney Ellis. But it was almost the last flicker of a dying fire.

Presently there was only Mr. Style, more bent, his beard now snowy-white. Then he was seen in Hope Street no more, and his place was taken by a German, Otto Baier. But his ministry was short-lived and he preached to empty pews.

In 1941 a club for Norwegian seamen was established in the basement of the whilom Temple.

Finally, on October 19th, 1947, the old building was rededicated to become the Third Church of Christ Scientist. The statue was removed. The last trace of the Positivists had faded away.

Now there is nothing—nothing except that empty alcove twenty or so feet up on the red brick face of an unobtrusive church on the darker side of Upper Parliament Street . . .

*A WELL-WATERED meander
on a rainy day when a hazel-twig
would have served better than
an umbrella, and how the water-
wagon had finally to be abandoned
in favour of ale.*

TO EARTH IN SEARCH OF WATER

WHAT was really needed was a diviner with one of those wonderful cavorting rods, instead I had to have recourse to sundry old and dry records in my quest for cool clear water.

It was a pouring wet day when I set out and had I told anyone that I was searching for water it would have been inviting a very rude reply, but the fact was that I was hunting around for some of Liverpool's hidden wells.

To-day when, with no more effort than the turning of a tap, we can obtain as much water as we wish, we tend to take that very necessary commodity rather for granted, but time was when it was so scarce and valuable that folk had to buy, beg, borrow and have even been known to steal it.

In the early days when Liverpool was still little more than a fishing village, water-supply did not constitute a serious problem, for the city is built on sandstone, a rock which holds water like a gigantic sponge. All you had to do was sink a well and you could be reasonably sure of finding a plentiful amount of good fresh water.

Many of these haphazard wells still exist to-day, and hunting for them can be quite a fascinating pursuit. Most frequently they come to light when old property is being demolished. When, for example, in 1931 a large part of North John Street was being rebuilt, clearing operations revealed five old circular wells, each some 5 feet in diameter, cut into the solid red sandstone and going down 35-40 feet. In 1927 excavations for the Mersey Tunnel penetrated the lower reaches of an old well situated below the Albany, Old Hall Street, and in 1936 when Radiant House was being erected in Bold Street three ancient wells were discovered. Two of them were bone-dry, but the third yielded water which was actually used by the builders in the work of construction.

At various times chance discoveries of wells have been reported from all over Liverpool—Hilbre Street, Jenner Street, Landseer Road, Mill Street, Oxford Street, Park Road, Rose Vale, Upper Parliament Street and Wynnstay Street, to name a few.

Occasionally one stumbles on—or maybe into—such wells in somewhat alarming circumstances. Back in July 1938, a woman walking through a narrow passageway opposite Conway Street, near Great Homer Street, screamed as she felt the ground giving beneath her feet. She had crossed the 8-foot-wide top of a hitherto unsuspected well. One June day in 1933 a lorry carrying a load of demolition debris away from the old premises of the Mumford Smith Brewery, situated between Highfield Street and Upper Milk Street, came to a sudden standstill with one of its front wheels sunk into the mouth of a 140-foot well. Again, in 1892, in the front area of a house at the corner of Huskisson and Catharine streets, the tenant discovered a gaping hole in a spot where, a few minutes before, her children had been playing. The timber supports of the cover of an old well, 70 feet deep, had fallen in.

*　*　*　*

Apart from such privately-owned wells, there was a number of public wells and springs.

I went in search of two of the most famous of these—the Fall Well and Gregson's Well.

The Fall Well was fed by a natural spring which surfaced on the Great Heath and had existed there from time immemorial. Enclosed by square stone walls, surrounded by low stone benches, covered by rude stone arches and topped with a stone cross, the name 'Fall' was probably given to the well because of the abrupt fall of the land thereabouts. It was the chief source of water-supply at the east end of the town, and when it was filled in, somewhere about 1790, its water was diverted to a fountain in the garden of William Roe (whose name is commemorated by Roe Street), the site of which is now occupied by the Stork Hotel. Nothing remains of the Fall Well to-day, but its waters once bubbled to the surface at some spot close to Rylands Buildings in Lime Street.

Gregson's Well has likewise vanished. Even its site is in considerable dispute. Once, protected by a graceful iron palisade, it gurgled away at the foot of some moss-grown steps, a few yards from the front gate of Mr. Gregson's villa on the corner of Everton Road.

The best I could find were two public-houses bearing its name, both of which claim to occupy the place of the well. In each of these I took a glass of something a deal more palatable than well-water with the hospitable landlord. The proprietor of the house on the Everton Road and Radcliffe Street corner, Mr. M. J. Byrne, showed me a very old and rather splendid oil-painting of the well which hangs in his public bar. Liberally gilded, it depicts a child with a pitcher seated beside a well, the water from which gushes out of a Romanesque mask. Across the way, the landlord, Mr. John Neary, took me down into his cellar and showed me . . . a sandstone well ! We neither of us thought, however, that it was *the* well. And just to complicate matters, Mr. Neary told me that nineteen years ago a well was uncovered by workmen excavating the premises of Messrs. Ferguson & Harvey a few yards away at the top of Low Hill. Personally, I am convinced that a third old well, which was discovered during the digging of the foundations of the Midland Bank on the corner of Radcliffe Street, and which caused a good deal of trouble as the water kept welling up, was the genuine article.

★　　★　　★　　★

Nowadays when much of Liverpool's daily water consumption of about 40 million gallons comes from an artificial lake in the heart of the Welsh mountains—Lake Vyrnwy—it seems a far cry from the time when the growing town relied upon wells, and when water-carts, driven by Amazonian women, hawked tin-cans of water from door to door. It seems incredible to read advertisements such as that which appeared two hundred years ago in a Liverpool newspaper : " At Edmund Parker's pump, on Shaw's Brow, may be had water at 9d. per butt." But it is most incredible of all to think that it was less than a hundred years ago that Liverpool for the first time in her history enjoyed the benison of a continuous and abundant supply of cool clear water.

*WITH quirks and points, punches
and boasters, twenty-three men
of stone give good account of
themselves and raise a monument
to heaven.*

BANKERS ON MOUNT ZION

TWELVE craftsmen and eleven apprentices are carving their way into immortality at the foot of Mount Zion.

Mount Zion, in case you didn't know, is the old name (which you will find on Perry's Liverpool map of 1769) for St. James's Mount. The Mount is an artificial hill and its formation dates back to 1767. At that time the lip of the great quarry at the top of Duke Street was an unsightly mass of earth, rock and rubbish which had been thrown up in the course of the excavations. The winter of 1767-8 was an exceptionally severe one, and the mayor, Mr. Thomas Johnson, observing that " the price of bread was high and the sufferings of the poor were great " was " animated by a benevolent desire to mitigate their sufferings by affording employment."

Accordingly, he suggested to the council that they should undertake the task of forming all this rubble into a single well-proportioned hill. The council agreed and the eminence which was christened Mount Zion came into being. On the completion of the Mount, a terrace, fronted by a smooth green slope, was constructed along the extent of the quarry and, on the crown of the hill, a beautiful little pleasure-garden and plantation were laid out.

In later years the plantation boasted an extensive rookery which was said to have been originated by a citizen who, seeing a pair of magpies building in one of the trees, clambered up and placed a couple of rook's eggs in their nest, and the magpies obligingly hatched them out.

The pleasure-garden was a great success. Commanding a magnificent prospect across the valley of rooftops, spires and domes of the town to the silver-flecked river and purple hills of Wales, it rapidly became one of the most popular promenades in Liverpool.

Possibly with the idea of recouping some of the money which their little exercise in charity had cost them, the corporation decided to lease part of the Mount for building purposes, and a row of houses was erected along what is now St. James's Road. It was as a direct result of this that Mount Zion vanished from the map.

It came about in this way. One of the houses was converted into a tavern which, with its large garden and pleasant situation, soon developed into a favourite resort. The association—even nominal—of anything so unhallowed as a public-house with Mount Zion disturbed some sensitive consciences of the day, and so, with the building of St. James's Church in 1774, Mount Zion was renamed St. James's Walk. In 1904 Mount Zion was appropriately selected as the site for Liverpool's great new Anglican cathedral.

*　*　*　*

One day recently I made pilgrimage to Mount Zion, where for more than half a century, through two world wars and three generations of craftsmen, work has never stopped on the raising of this three-million-pound monument to God.

Back in 1939, 120 masons shaped its stones. To-day there are only a dozen, and eleven apprentices—though that, said the foreman, is more apprentices than have ever been employed here before.

Every month 600 cubic feet of random rock come to the Mount from Woolton's sandstone quarries. When it arrives the rough stone may go through the frame-saw to be reduced to slabs of more manageable size, or it may go direct to the quarrymen for ' scabbling ' (that is to have the large rough pieces knocked off) but every single stone, from monsters weighing five tons to the tiny pinnacle pieces, has eventually to pass through the hands of the masons.

*　*　*　*

It is the masons' shed that is the real birthplace of the cathedral, and there, each at his stool, or banker as it is officially called, I met some of the men and boys who, with quirks and points, punches, boasters and inch tools, are carrying on the age-old craft of the stone-mason—men like 72-year-old Harry James, a master craftsman who prides himself on never having had a job brought back as unsatisfactory in fifty-six years as a mason. Mr. James has been lending his skill to the building of Liverpool Cathedral for thirty-six years now. He is, perhaps, nearing the end of his working life, but at a banker close beside him I met 15-year-old Donald Holland. He is at the very beginning of his career—" I started nine months ago," he told me, " and I hope to be here to see the last stone dressed and put in place."

" That lad's going to be a *real* mason," the foreman confided. " The apprentice of to-day is every bit as good as his father and grand-

136

father providing he's keen, and never you let anyone tell you different."

I noticed that some of the pieces of stone had initials carved on them. "Those are the banker-marks," I was told. "You probably know them as mason's marks." In the old days they were secret signs used by itinerant masons and devised for the mutual recognition of each other as experts in the art, and not mere imposters. You will find ancient mason's marks on the stonework of many an old building in the vicinity of Liverpool, such as Sefton Church, Aughton Church, Ormskirk Church, Burscough Priory and Stonyhurst College. The old masons, who could neither read nor write, used devices like arrows and crosses. Nowadays, a mason frequently uses his own initials.

And standing there in the masons' shed, seeing the men at work in their aprons—"Not all masons wear the calico apron these days. Some of them wear overalls and look more like engineers," said Mr. James disdainfully—using their beechwood mallets and that proud symbol of the craft, the square, I could not help remembering that great and noble movement which is reputed to have found its inspiration in just such sheds where worked the men who built Solomon's Temple.

*   *   *   *

I took my last look at the masons from the very peak of Mount Zion. Three hundred and thirty-one feet up, on the crest of the cathedral, I gazed down at the tiny figures in the yard below. It seemed incredible that those minute, moving specks should have been responsible for the erection of this vast aerial platform.

I saw the mallets strike the winking silver of the chisel-heads, but heard no sound—only the roaring of the wind. I thought of the legions of former hands—banker hands and mason fixers—who had shaped and carried each of those millions of stones. And then I looked down again. There, in the late afternoon sun, twelve crafts-men and eleven apprentices busy about work that will endure for perhaps two thousand years . . . maybe much longer . . .

ON Saturday night the town hums,
but it is in a windowless shell
suspended in space that the music
of Liverpool sounds.

THERE IS SWEET MUSIC HERE

SEVEN-THIRTY on a Saturday night.

The bright-coloured top that is town beginning to spin.

Queues of those who like to purchase their pleasure ready-made line the twinkling streets and curl about the cinemas and theatres.

In restaurant and public-house thousands of others are busying themselves forging their own more personal fun.

Up the dark slope of Hardman Street, insulated within the clean-lined brick building that crests the hill, 1,900 music-loving Merseysiders voyage happily on a sea of sound.

Beyond those walls the Saturday-night town hums, but it is here in the Philharmonic Hall that the real music of Liverpool is played—now louder than the roar of all the city's traffic, now soft as the whisper of waves picking the old sea-wall.

I sit in the stalls and let my eyes wander. Away from the platform with its black-and-white patina of musicians, ranged like chessmen, its stained wood and shining brass; away from the weaving baton, conducting and controlling in the maestro's hand, my gaze steals furtively along the quiet, rapt rows. Here a young face flushed with discovery; there an old face tranquil with remembrance. An elderly lady leans back in her seat with closed eyes. A young man with unruly hair is bent forward over the open score on his lap. Two teenage girls sit clasping hands, their lips slightly apart. And all around and about us the music, stirring as many responsive chords as there are listeners in the audience.

★   ★   ★   ★

For 108 years now there has been music at the top of Hardman Street, for it was in August 1849 that the Liverpool Philharmonic Society, which had been founded nine years previously by a group of

Liverpool gentlemen with the avowed intention of co-ordinating and extending musical interests in the city, opened its first concert hall on the site of the present Philharmonic Hall.

In the early days concerts were much longer than they are to-day. Glancing through some of the old programmes I saw that it was by no means unusual for the first half alone to include an overture, a concerto and a full symphony, together with a liberal sprinkling of arias, the entire performance occupying anything up to four hours. Nowadays a concert generally lasts about two hours, and that includes an interval for the taking of coffee or maybe something stronger.

There have been other changes, too. Once upon a time no one would be admitted to a concert unless wearing full evening-dress. From where I was sitting I could see a number of men in sports jackets and flannels and at least three young women in slacks.

*   *   *   *

It may have been because at this point the music suddenly took on a mood of savage grandeur, that I found myself wondering how many twentieth-century concert-goers realise that every time they go to listen to music they are assisting at a rite which is almost as old as man himself.

Experts estimate that for fully 25,000 years men and women have surrendered themselves to the pleasure of patterned sound. Music began in the jungle and the swamp, and though it is a long stretch from the first drums and rattles used in ancient fertility rites and primitive obsequies to sun and moon, to the euphonious and highly skilled music of modern times, basic principles have changed little. The thunder of Beethoven, the complex melodic threads of Bach and the bucolic gaiety of Haydn all depend upon the blowing, scraping and banging of wood, bone, metal, goat-skins, sheep's guts and bits of bamboo. There is indeed something ageless about music. It diminishes space and time as no other art can. Its melodies stem from every country. Its listeners are often tuned in to wavelengths of sound created a couple of hundred years ago. This quality of timelessness is emphasised by the very structure of the new Philharmonic Hall, which in 1939 replaced the old hall, burned down in July 1933, for, incredibly, the entire shell of the auditorium is suspended in space, slung from the roof of the outer building. Moreover, the atmosphere within that shell is most definitely timeless for, entirely without windows, it excludes the external world of day and night.

*   *   *   *

It was in the greenroom that, during the interval, I was shown two great leather-bound volumes between whose covers is preserved a large slice of the history of what is among the half-dozen oldest musical societies in the world.   These books are crammed with a series of photographs, many of them signed with fading fanfares of eccentric copperplate, of the musically great who have graced our city with their artistry—Jenny Lind, Paderewski, Melba, Tetrazzini, Patti and a host of others.   It was not without a certain pride that I discovered on the very first page of the first volume a photograph of my own great-grandfather, James Zeugheer-Herrmann, the Philharmonic Society's first resident conductor.

But it is not as a museum, nor even because of the excellence of the coffee that one can drink there, that the greenroom is important. It is because of the lively part which it plays in the cultural life of Liverpool.   There, on concert nights, guests from many different professions and branches of art and commerce are invited to meet one another and be introduced to the conductor and the artists.

⋆   ⋆   ⋆   ⋆

It was just after 9-30 when the concert finished.   Out into the night and down the hill spilled the audience.   As I watched them go they seemed a strangely-assorted crowd.   Now and again I caught a snatch of conversation.   " But, my dear, Tchaikovsky's Fifth—it's HEAVEN.   You simply *must* know it."   " Well, darling, personally I just *adore* Mozart."   Some spoke just a semitone too loudly, but on the whole I am sure that they were sincere enough.   I am sure, too, that each and every one of them appreciated to the full the magic of music— that strange power it has of transporting our own little sufferings into the realms of majestic tragedy and setting a seal of greatness upon our equally insignificant triumphs.

*BEING the vehicle for a
hotchpotch of oddities collected
one lunch-hour in the city streets.*

THE CURIOUS PERAMBULATOR

A LMOST as soon as I had learned to read, a great-aunt of mine
made me a present of a book called *Eyes and No Eyes*. It
was written by an elderly Victorian lady with a passion for
natural history, and so admirably did it fulfil its professed purpose of
" teaching the quality of observation to the young," that, ever since,
I have gone through life with eyes more than usually wide open, and
have in consequence noticed many of those things which G. K.
Chesterton called " tremendous trifles," and which it is so easy—
and such a pity—to miss.

Let me give you just a few random examples of the results of a
bout of this eyes-and-no-eyes game which I found myself playing during a lunch-hour perambulation which extended from the Pier Head
to St. George's Hall.

*   *   *   *

My first discovery was a monument raised to the memory of a
Liverpool café proprietor in 1885—Simpson's Bowl, a small stone
fountain affixed to the wall of St. Nicholas's Church at the corner
of George's Dock Gates and Chapel Street.

Of all the thousands who must pass that little fountain with its
metal relief sculpture of Mr. Simpson's luxuriantly-bewhiskered head,
how many, I wonder, know the story which it commemorates ?

It is a charitable and inspiring tale.

William Simpson was, during the latter years of the 19th
century, the proprietor of the famous Landing-Stage Café.

A tall eccentric-looking man with an immense drooping
mustachio, he was a colourful character who, with his invariable
cigar and coruscant diamond scarf-pin, set in the midst of a gleaming
expanse of shirt-front, compelled the attention of all who saw him.

Far from being discomfited by the stares of lesser mortals, he seems to have relished the stir he caused and proclaimed it his aim " never to do anything that an ordinary person does."

He made several bids to enter politics. Despite the handicap of a thin harsh voice, he was a powerful and persuasive orator, and in 1874 fought the general election as a Liberal-Conservative. Much to his disappointment he lost, but five years later he stood for the West Derby ward at the municipal election. This time he won, but shortly afterwards lost his seat on the council because he lived over his café on the landing-stage and was not therefore either a ratepayer or a resident in Liverpool.

It was during the time of the terrible Indian famine of 1877-8 that Simpson first conceived the idea of placing an open brass bowl on the landing-stage into which passers-by might cast a copper or two's worth of their charity. The result exceeded all expectations. Within thirty-one days £203 1s. 3d. had found its way into Simpson's Bowl.

Subsequently pressed into service for the relief of the distressed miners of South Wales, the victims of the Haydock Colliery accident, the Liverpool Distress Fund, the Irish Distress Fund and the Abercarn Colliery Accident Fund, the bowl collected in all the sum of £3,515 1s. 8½d. in cash, and a further £1,250 worth of food and clothing was heaped about it in boxes, bales and bundles.

Simpson died on June 16th, 1883. His widow and three daughters —Violet, Bonnie and Ivy—continued to live above the café on the landing-stage well into the present century. They eventually moved to Llandudno where they opened an hotel.

Although the stone basin of the St. Nicholas fountain is sometimes referred to as Simpson's Bowl, it is not, of course, the original. That was presented by the family to Liverpool Corporation, and it is now preserved in the Town Clerk's Department of the Municipal Offices where its charitable lustre outshines many a more intrinsically valuable piece of civic plate.

*　　*　　*　　*

Continuing my stroll up Chapel Street and along Covent Garden, where a polished brass plate within the doorway of the " Pig and Whistle," bearing the legend " Emigrants Supplied," recalls the old dead days when weary Englishmen made Liverpool their springboard to adventuring across the seas, I came into Water Street, and crossed to the magnificent building of the National Provincial Bank where, literally upon its doorstep, I stumbled on one of the strangest stories of modern Liverpool.

On the doors of the bank are two great bronze tiger heads, and if you look at them closely you will see that the tops of the canine teeth are polished to an alien brightness. This is the result of many years of friction against dark palms, for this bank door is a place of pilgrimage. In far-off India they know all about the twin tigers of Liverpool, and among native seamen it has become a tradition to pay a respectful visit to them. So if, some moonlight night, you see a dark figure slip quietly up Water Street from the direction of the waterfront, pause and rub his hand across the teeth of a brazen tiger, do not be surprised. He is no potential bank robber but a pilgrim from the Land of the Tiger, and he is only making his harmless obeisances to the god of Luck.

* * * *

After crossing Castle Street, where I paused to look at the Sanctuary Stone, one of the boundary stones of the old Liverpool Fair (within the precincts of which debtors coming to the fair on lawful business were guaranteed freedom from arrest for a period of ten days before and after the fair), which is embedded in the road just opposite the premises of the Westminster Bank, I made a short detour into Sweeting Street to see the only one of Liverpool's 34,000 or so street lamps which burns all day and is extinguished at night. This unique lamp is actually situated in a passageway inside an office building through which there is free access to Union Court, and at night when the building is closed and the clerks and typists are snug in their suburban dormitories its flickering yellow flame is doused.

* * * *

My stroll began at a fountain and it ended by one—beside the Steble Fountain opposite St. George's Hall, where, close to the base of the Wellington Column, you may see Liverpool's measuring stone. It is marked out with iron pegs : one foot, two feet, imperial yard. And on a heavy iron plate bolted to the black stone-work is inscribed : " Standard measures at 62 Fahrenheit verified by the Standards Department Board of Trade."

And after that I walked fifty yards to see Beethoven's piano . . . but that's another story . . .

*IT'S 'No Smoking' here, but
a hundred tons of ripe gold 'baccy
are consumed every year by
the three-foot bowl of the
monarch's mammoth pipe.*

THE KING'S PIPE

D URING the past six months fifty tons of tobacco have gone curling up in rich pungent smoke to the grey Liverpool skies. Fifty tons of ripe gold 'baccy, representing, at current prices, a round £300,000, crammed into the hungry three-foot bowl of the ' King's Pipe.' And myself, an enthusiastic pipeman, ignorant of the very existence of this Gargantuan ' pipe ' until, a day or two ago, I stood beside it in the destruction shed of the Stanley Tobacco Warehouse here in Liverpool, and saw a rueful warehouseman feeding sack after sack of yellow Virginia leaf to the flames.

★   ★   ★   ★

" No smoking, please," the official in charge had said to me as I presented myself at the carefully-guarded gate of the biggest warehouse on earth.

" No smoking, please," said the manager as he prepared to escort me on a two-mile tour of the 36 tobacco-packed acres of the great Mersey Docks and Harbour Board warehouse over which he presides, and I carefully emptied my pipe, matches and tobacco-pouch out onto his desk before he led me across the cobbled yard to where the mighty, 125-foot warehouse reared like a gigantic fortress into the air.

" Seven hundred and thirty feet long, 165 feet wide, 14 stories, 32 miles of electric wiring, 6,000 tons of iron and 27 million bricks ; it dwarfs St. George's Hall," said my escort with enthusiasm.

Built, in 1900, at a cost of nearly half a million pounds, by that same firm which is raising Liverpool Cathedral, the Stanley Tobacco Warehouse is surely one of the wonders of the modern world, a worthy essay in the superlative tradition of a city that also boasts, besides the largest electrically-driven clock in England, the largest organ, the largest grain silos and the largest floating structure (Prince's Landing-Stage) in the world.

" No Smoking," ordered notices inside the warehouse where we walked, literally for miles, through avenues of casks, cases and bales brimful with more than £200,000,000 worth of tobacco. Tobacco from America, Africa, India, Canada, Turkey, Greece, Cyprus, Italy, Cuba, Latakia, Bulgaria, Java and Sumatra—35,000 tons of it.

" Each of those casks is worth £3,000," said my guide. " That is, of course, taking the duty into account. Actually, you can reckon that when the tobacco comes in here it is valued at about five shillings a pound, but by the time it leaves us it is up to 63 shillings the pound."

As we mounted slowly up the fourteen floors, each of which could comfortably accommodate half a dozen full-scale football matches simultaneously, I reflected that just one of those 70,000 casks could set me up very nicely, and I began to understand why police and customs watchers are continually patrolling and keeping hawk-like eyes on the precious leaf.

Upstairs on the top floor are the scales which form the nerve-centre of the entire warehouse. Every cask, case and bale that is delivered is lugged up here (" Because the glass roof affords a better light.") where it is opened, the contents emptied out and carefully weighed under the scrutiny of a customs officer and a Dock-Board official who sit in two little wooden cabins. " The beam scales may look old-fashioned," I was told, " but they are the most accurate weighing machines in Liverpool." They are tested at least four times a day. You have to be very careful when a mistake may cost you hundreds of pounds. Duly weighed, the tobacco is packed back into its cask and the whole place echoes to the rappings of the coopers' hammers. Each cask is then marked and stowed away in one or other of the eighty-four vast storerooms. Any tobacco which has been spilled during weighing operations is immediately swept up and placed in special sacks. I examined a quantity of this crude leaf and remarked to my guide that this must be the sort of tobacco that Sir Walter Raleigh started the whole thing off with. How wrong I was. He promptly produced a small book from his pocket and in it I read that the particular weed that Raleigh favoured was of a crude and coarse kind which is only cultivated on a small scale to-day and is used mainly for the manufacture of nicotine as an insecticide ! The pipe that is said to have soothed Sir Walter Raleigh's last hours would be more likely to reconcile a condemned man to his fate in these days.

*　　*　　*　　*

It was still ' No Smoking ' in the 100-year-old shed in a corner of the warehouse yard that houses the ' King's Pipe.' The ' King's Pipe ' is a very special furnace in which all the tobacco sweepings, condemned leaf and confiscated cigarettes are burned.

" Surely," I said, " it should be called the ' Queen's Pipe ' now ? " But, no. Apparently, this old furnace is one of the very few things which does *not* change its designation with that of the sovereign.

In the shed I met 61-year-old Bob Smith, the custodian of the ' Pipe.' Bob smokes very little himself—he sucks peppermints. " The ' Pipe ' smokes enough for both of us ," he laughed. Puff, puff, puff, every day from 8 a.m., when he kindles it, until 4 p.m. when he extinguishes it. And, as the tall brick chimney scents the air, the locals sniff appreciatively and say : " The King's having a good smoke to-day."

It was the delicious aroma of that monarchal pipe that brought our most edifying tour to a somewhat abrupt end. Without another word we fled to the manager's office . . . for a smoke !

SOME account of an impossible quest for a non-existent avian which ended successfully in the gentlemen's cloak-room of the Town hall.

STALKING THE LIVER BIRD

HAVING just spent a breathless June day in hopeless quest of the fabulous Liver Bird I am able to state categorically that ornithological invention is not the prerogative of Carroll, Lear and Araby. Jubjub, tropical turnspit and roc are no more and no less nonsuch, never-were birds than Herodotus's Phoenix and Liverpool's Liver.

I speak with authority for, seizing my runcible hat and slinging a pair of powerful bird-watching binoculars across my shoulders, I have hied me to the concrete forests of the streets and searched high and low for the elusive Liver.

In the course of my hunt I found carvings and pictures of the Liver Bird in abundance ; on the green belly of the bus that bore me townwards ; on the façades of sundry buildings and on the paper and furniture of municipal officialdom ; but it was in the quiet groves of the Picton that I discovered the first feathers as it were of the Liver.

But alas ! Grim discovery. Those feathers belonged to an eagle —the eagle of St. John—and as I turned sheaf after sheaf of musty papers it became more and more painfully obvious that the Liver Bird was a myth, hatched, centuries ago, out of an eagle's egg.

*   *   *   *

It was in the year 1207 that King John, desiring a port from which to embark military supplies to Ireland, granted letters patent to Liverpool, and, twenty-two years later, his son, Henry III, gave Liverpool a charter constituting it a free borough. Anxious to celebrate its new-found freedom, the town promptly decided to adopt a corporate seal, and it may be that the eagle of St. John was chosen in judicious compliment to the House of King John—a supposition to which substance is lent by the fact that the eagle held in its beak a sprig of the Plantagenet emblem, the *planta genista* (broom pods and leaves). The seal would be made of either silver or brass—most likely silver—and only one good wax impression of it survives. It is in the muniment room at Croxteth Hall.

Liverpool lost this first seal during the siege of 1644 when Prince Rupert's troops sacked the town and carried off its plate. It was, however, replaced in 1655 by a second seal of silver (which is still in use) engraved with a bird which, because of inferior workmanship, bore not the slightest resemblance to the Evangelist's eagle. Indeed, as the centuries wore on, this somewhat nondescript bird came to be regarded as a hen cormorant which, considering the large numbers of cormorants which disport themselves in the Mersey, is scarcely surprising.

Perhaps it is not quite fair to lay all the blame for the disappearance of the eagle at the door of the unskilful engraver, for as far back as 1611 the town records were speaking of the Liverpool bird as a cormorant. The first authentic allusion to anything approaching a Liver Bird occurs in 1668 when the then Earl of Derby presented the municipality with a mace engraved with " a leaver." By April 25th, 1743, the old seal, stolen practically a century before by Prince Rupert, had been recovered by the Corporation, and on that date an order was made that the *new* seal should be destroyed.

Due to some unfortunate mistake, however, it was the old seal that was destroyed, on October 14th, 1743, and consequently the *new* seal continues in use to this day.

In 1796 a horrified town-council suddenly discovered that Liverpool had in fact no ratified arms, and representations were hastily made to the College of Arms. One Alderman Clayton Tarleton was empowered to negotiate on behalf of the Corporation, and he suggested to the College that the proper bird to adorn Liverpool's crest was a " Lever or Sea Cormorant." The Heralds decided, however, that it should be a plain cormorant and specified that it should hold a branch of laver in its bill. That the bird on the old seal was intended for an eagle—the eagle of St. John—is made abundantly clear by the inscription, " Johannis," which appears below it. Indeed, when arms were granted to the Bishopric of Liverpool in 1882 the bird was properly shown as an eagle. Thus, we have to-day the curious situation of the arms of the bishopric correctly bearing an eagle, while the arms of the Corporation are erroneously emblazoned with an ornithologically suspect cormorant.

*   *   *   *

After digesting all this I never expected to find a stuffed Liver Bird in Liverpool. But I did. It was in the basement cloak-room of the Town hall. " Once upon a time," I was told, " it stood in its glass case at the foot of the stairs, but a former Lord Mayor who had no taste for such things ordered its removal and it was hurriedly stowed away downstairs." I took with me a friend learned in ornithology. He glanced at it and pronounced : " It is a young cormorant." Rumour has it that this is the actual specimen which, in 1796, was despatched to the College of Arms to show them exactly what a " Lever or Sea Cormorant " looked like. My friend, an expert in such matters, said that of course it was *possible*, but we decided that it was far more likely that some nineteenth-century, know-all alderman had said to his Lord Mayor : " I tell you there *was* such a bird as the Liver Bird, and what is more I have one and will bring it to show you." We pictured the scene. One day the bird, carefully stuffed, was lugged along to the Town hall. The city fathers stood around in wonderment. " Well it certainly *looks* like the Liver Bird," ventured one a trifle more naïve than the rest. " I tell you it *is* the Liver Bird "—this, somewhat exasperatedly, from its owner. " Well, well, I never thought I'd live to see a stuffed Liver Bird," the Lord Mayor would say shaking his head. " It'd be all right to have it in the mayor's parlour," someone would rashly suggest. That was all that was needed. Its triumphant owner was delighted to make the gesture and Liverpool was duly given the bird.

*   *   *   *

Leaving the cormorant in the cellar, I made my way to the Liver Building and climbed 483 steps to the veritable eyrie of the Liver Bird. Three hundred odd feet up I came out from a tunnel of brick onto the windswept roof of Liverpool, and above me I saw the two 18-foot Liver Birds. There they stood, glinting green in the sunlight, their wings raised as though alerted for flight. Standing in that lonely place I had the feeling that at any moment they might wing their way off, out across the estuary to the Never-Never Land from which they came. But, happily, they moved not a metal feather, for have the wiseacres not said that the day the Liver Birds fly away, that day will see the end of Liverpool ?

*WHY Liverpool gentlemen pull
out their watches and the Pier Head
pigeons take wing every day,
except Sunday, at 1 p.m. precisely.*

LIVERPOOL'S DAILY BANG

SINCE first it awoke the echoes and scattered the pigeons of
Merseyside on September 21st, 1867, the boom of the One-o'Clock
Gun has become so much a part of the pattern of Liverpool
life that we seldom seem to think of it. Only the stranger discovers
anything odd in the sound of a sharp report followed by a street
scene of elderly gentlemen pausing to draw forth their gold hunters,
and young men shooting out their wrists in unison. And yet the
average Merseysider is as vague regarding the history and workings
of the time-gun as I myself proved when, the other day, a friend,
briefly here from London, gave me pause with a salvo of questions
concerning the daily bang to which my ears since childhood have
grown accustomed.

*   *   *   *

The origin of the One-o'Clock Gun is closely tied up with the
story of Liverpool as one of the great maritime centres of England.
A century ago this city of ours was famed for the excellence of the
ships' chronometers which were manufactured here. Now an essential
part of the stock-in-trade of the manufacturers of such instruments
is a very accurate means of measuring time, and it was the daily custom
of the chronometer makers to repair at one o'clock to the old Liverpool
Observatory at Waterloo Dock in order to check their timepieces.
When, in 1867, the observatory was moved over the water to Bidston
Hill, the chronometer makers were exceedingly disgruntled until
John Hartnup, the then director of the observatory, had the bright
idea of firing off a time-signal, by means of which they would still
be able to get the correct time from him, at one o'clock each day.
An ancient 34-pounder cannon, which had seen service in the Crimean
and earlier wars, was secured and installed on Morpeth Pier Head.

This gun, which was set off from Bidston Observatory by means of an electric connection, was at first fired with 7 lbs. of powder, but as it frequently shattered windows in Birkenhead and, incredibly, a number in Everton, the charge was subsequently reduced to 5 lbs.

The gun continued in daily use—Sundays, bank-holidays, Christmas Day and Good Friday excepted—right up to 1932, though it was nearly spiked in the October of that year when the Marine Committee of the Mersey Docks and Harbour Board, whose responsibility it is, recommended that the time-honoured signal should be abandoned. At that time the old gun had been condemned by the ordnance authorities and a reserve gun brought into use, but the Committee felt that now that constant radio time-signals had become the order of the day the expense of maintaining the gun—then about £100 a year—was not justified. The public, however, came down heavily on the side of the gun and the Committee withdrew its recommendation. The War Office intimated its willingness to supply a new gun at trifling cost and, on April 26th, 1933, a 32-pounder of similar construction to the original one arrived from Woolwich Arsenal, and the old cannon was rusticated to grace a quiet lawn at Bidston Observatory.

This second gun continued in loud service right up to September 1st, 1939, when a six-and-a-half-year security silence was imposed on it for the duration of the Second World War. In October 1945, a proposal was put forward to resume the time-signal. A third gun, this time a Hotchkiss 6-pounder naval gun, was set up in Birkenhead, and on June 17th, 1946, the old familiar bang reverberated once again across the waters of the Mersey.

*   *   *   *

At 12-29 one sunny morning I stood before an innocent-looking clock—rather like one of those grandfathers of a bygone age—in the central room of Bidston Observatory. Beside me was the young girl whose job it was that day to fire the One-o'Clock Gun. One minute before she had sent a careful time-check to Morpeth Dock, and now she was about to test the electric circuit which is completed when two slender wires are brought almost into contact within the head of the fuse to fire the gun. Watching the second-hand creep slowly up towards the sixtieth mark, it seemed strange to reflect that once in every twenty-four hours that almost soundless clock, which neither strikes nor very audibly ticks, makes such a noise in the world. At 12-30 precisely, down went the switch and the quivering needles on a nearby control panel told us that $3\frac{1}{2}$ miles away in the water-front gun-house the trigger had clicked down. The dummy fire, the daily dress-rehearsal without music, had been successfully completed.

Landing-Stage Seaman Alf Harris was just filling the shell with its 15 oz. bag of powder as, after a breathless dash to Morpeth Pier, I scrambled up the steel ladder and edged my way carefully past the projecting grey muzzle of the One-o'Clock Gun into the little brick-built gun-house. At 12-50 he loaded the blank shell into the breach of the gun and carefully opened all the windows of the hut— " It's rather restricted quarters for an explosion, you'd better keep your mouth open when she fires," he told me. By 12-59 the atmosphere was, so far as I was concerned anyway, decidedly tense. Seaman Harris pulled the switches to the observatory down. We all waited for the big bang, praying that nothing would go wrong. Six times in eighty-nine years the gun has failed to fire. Once, on July 20th, 1915, she fired twice and, scandal, on July 11th, 1935, she fired 35 seconds late. Mr. Harris stood by with a small stick ready to depress the trigger-release should the automatic mechanism go wrong. At 1 o'clock exactly there was a terrific explosion, a blue flash. I felt a thwack of warm air on my legs, the place filled with the sudden stench of cordite. A puff of grey pigeons rose high into the air and through my singing ears I heard the sirens wail acknowledgement of our timely service.

*A FORAGE in that rotund biblio-
theca whose voluminous alcoves
shelter double elephants, and
whither a dignified lady betook
herself to inquire as to the correct
time for cutting capers.*

READERS' RETREAT

DOMED, like the round skull of an intellectual, looms the rotund
bulk of the Picton Reference Library—Liverpool's Temple of
Literature.

Outside, on this bitter February day, a powder of snow sets a
white wig on its bald black brow. Inside, a centrally-heated silence
in which the whisperings of resentfully-parting pages raise a sibilance
of echoes. It is as if, high in the Pantheonic dome, the Muses conspire
upon which bent head they will bestow wisdom.

But for all its silence this is a battleground ; the restless front of
learning. And, bearing their battle-scars of lined brows and red
myopic eyes, the warriors sit in radiating rows of desks, ordered or
disordered as their minds, the bent heads of senility and the challeng-
ing heads of youth.

Here is Hope : a young girl, bright, pert and clear-eyed, screwing
a truant curl about her finger as she wrestles with a stout treatise on
mathematics. There, next to her, is Resignation : an old white-
bearded man in a velvet skull-cap, covering page after page with a
spider scrawl of notes culled from a big black leather volume.

And so it has been ever since 1879 when this great library, built
out of public funds and named after Sir James Allanson Picton, the
Liverpool historian and at that time chairman of the Library, Museum
and Arts Committee, first opened its doors.

Across the years the young have sought and found knowledge
in this vast book-lined rotunda. Age has here consolidated experience.
And here, too, some have suffered the death of youth and the strangu-
lation of belief. What a motley collection of habitués the place has
gathered to itself. They come and go like spectres :

Like Louis MacNeice's stooping haunted readers in the British Museum Reading Room.

*　　*　　*　　*

At one time or another some quest drives all of us to the quiet alcoves of the Picton—to turn yellowing archives in the local history section, to pin an elusive fact, to plant a genealogical tree, to uproot an old mystery. Here are the serried ranks of local newspapers, dating from 1756 : the rows of Liverpool directories, beginning at the year 1766. Upon miles of shelves, from floor to ceiling, and in thousands of tea-chests, deep from sight in hidden storerooms, are crammed more than a million items—books and pamphlets, maps and manuscripts. The oldest fragment of writing is a scrap of Liverpool's original Charter. Dated 1207, it is kept in a small glass-topped box. And in a fireproof safe is the Picton's most ancient printed book, a copy of Petrarch's " Sonnets," printed in Venice in 1407, which once graced the shelves of William Roscoe. The most valuable work in the library is Audubon's " Birds of America." It is worth more than £12,000. It has also the distinction of being the largest book in the Picton, each of its four volumes measuring fully three feet in height and nearly as much in width. Requiring two men to lift it comfortably, it is well-styled bibliographically a double elephant folio ! Side by side with this mammoth, I was shown the smallest book in the collection, a minute copy of the Koran scarcely larger than a postage-stamp. Bound in red, tooled with golden oriental designs, it nestles in a tiny chased silver case in the lid of which is inset a very necessary magnifying glass.

*　　*　　*　　*

The care and conservation of this huge and variegated collection of books is only one part of the duties of the staff. They must also be ever ready to help and guide the serious inquirer. Some of the inquiries are, to say the least, unusual. What is the origin of a chemist's coloured bottles ? Which part of the peacock was eaten in Roman times ? What was the etiquette and costume of the Portuguese court in Brazil between 1808 and 1830 ? A schoolgirl wants advice on making wigs for dolls. A lady would like to know the correct time for cutting capers. This last caused some perplexity until it was suddenly realised that she was referring to the plants in her garden !

And somehow or other all these awkward questions are answered, though sometimes, when the encyclopaedias and other learned tomes have failed to yield a solitary clue, the information turns up on the back of one of the cigarette-cards, a magnificent collection of which forms a cartophilist's corner of paradise in the gallery of a small back room.

★   ★   ★   ★

And so, day in day out (Sundays excepted), the reading and the searching go ceaselessly on from 9 a.m. to 9 p.m., when the gong shatters the day-long silence and sends the last lingering reader flitting out between the dusky pillars. Out from the steam-heated security of his bookish hideaway, past the pallid moon-washed statues into the frosty reality of the neon-hung night.

REMEMBERING those wilder shores of Aigburth where an ageing and monoculous lion was once wheeled out on sunny afternoons.

ON THE PROM

"VISIT Otterspool Promenade ", invited the poster in the bus, and when the sun came fitfully out I rose to the invitation. Four o'clock in the afternoon of one of the few light-hearted days of this sulky summer found me, together with a thousand or so other leisured Liverpudlians, taking the air beside the river.

In deference to a prim notice forbidding " Organised Games", bevies of children and coveys of yapping dogs chased haphazard india-rubber balls across shipshape ramps of turf. Amongst the flower-beds anxious mothers and fathers kept discreet vigil ; whilst, remote and withdrawn in a world of their own, the courting teenagers paraded, all blazers and print frocks. With unseeing eyes, an old man in a navy-blue suit, open-necked cricket-shirt and white tennis-shoes, gazed out across the river, on his knees a popular pin-up paper whose back was covered with a pencilling of recondite anagrammatic speculation.

It was all very formal and well behaved—a family party on a big scale—and lacked the brio of New Brighton whose supremacy as a Merseyside playground it challenges. For all its seven short years of life—and a beautifully-sculptured tablet inset in a wall commemorates the opening of the promenade on July 7th, 1950—it already has the settled look of a well-loved institution. Nature has indeed been tamed by the architect's blueprint and the landscape-gardener's trowel so successfully that I begin to doubt my own memories. Remembering the wilder shores that Aigburth presented to the river when I was a boy, I suddenly felt a little sad and very old. Did they ever exist, the rabbit-haunted cliffs of crumbling red clay, the Fisherman's Hut with its driftwood fence and its paper bags of shrimps, the wilderness of scrub and barbed wire which separated the romantic foreshore from the elegant gardens and parterres of the rambling gabled mansions of Aigburth's aristocracy ? Had I but known it, the future was shaping itself before my eyes as I watched through the whole of my childhood the endless procession of lorries trundling their loads of rubble and refuse down a steadily-widening Jericho Lane to form the first footings of that thrusting promenade.

Crossing a cindered car park to join a thirsty queue before a little wooden kiosk, I suddenly realised that I was treading upon a legend that I had cherished as a boy. The solid ground beneath my feet hid the cavern of a dock deep enough, we boys were told, to contain Mossley Hill Church, weathercock and all. It had been built, they said, during the 1914-18 war by a man who subsequently committed suicide. Two stories were told to account for his fate. You could believe either that he became desperate when the dock proved a commercial failure, or that he was a baffled German spy who made away with himself when his fell design of secreting enemy U-boats there was frustrated by an astute Secret Service. We were in no doubt as to which was true !

Refreshed by a cup of strong tea, I strolled through the open gate of Otterspool Park. It was a more dignified entrance to this pleasantly-wooded ravine than I was accustomed to making when I wore short trousers and was a little less portly. In those days a conveniently loose paling was gateway to the delights of Cross's Menagerie which was housed there. Under the awning of a somewhat jury-rigged bandstand, which irresistibly reminded me of the quarter-deck of a man o' war, a nautically-uniformed band played nostalgic selections from *Snow White*. It was to this precise spot that on long-ago summer afternoons an aged and agreeable lion with one eye used to be wheeled in a great perambulator of a cage, for all the world like a Boer-War general in retirement taking a constitutional in a Bath-chair. Where this noble brute's permanent prison was there is now a distinctly continental-looking café. It stands on the original terrace of the demolished mansion of the Moss family who formerly owned this estate. Some of the outbuildings have survived, and in the peeling coach-house, now used as a gardener's shed, there are still traces of its bizarre inhabitants during the Cross régime. Faded and barely legible, the eye of memory can still discern the legends : " Do Not Cross the Barrier " and " Do Not Tease the Monkeys." I regret to say that the balding badger and the two woebegone wolves (which we always secretly suspected of being Alsatians) have disappeared into Limbo leaving no memorials behind them.

*   *   *   *

And what of the pierrots who once set the valley ringing with *Shepherd of the Hills*, touchingly rendered for the sole benefit of two bedraggled small boys whom only an infinite pity for the performers kept out in the rain ? Clearly, the crowds, drugged with a surfeit of television and grown blasé with the superlatives of the cinema, who nowadays throng the terrace would not care for *that* sort of thing. Even the band, whose efforts I found quite delightful in an Edwardian kind of way, was given scant attention and less applause.

But for all that, Otterspool Park has, since the opening of the ' prom,' enjoyed a popularity which mysteriously eluded it before the war. Although on winter's nights, when the brisk westerly wind shakes the bright necklace of lights that adorns the promenade's bareness, there seems some substance in the carpings of the critics, my afternoon on the ' prom ' has convinced me that its conception was a good and wise move for Merseyside. And as for the romance that, for me, is fled, well maybe it is the departure of my youth rather than the coming of the concrete to the Aigburth waterfront that is to blame.

THE AMATEUR GUNMAN

9-35 p.m.

March 19th, 1949.

It was just an ordinary Saturday night. The usual audience of off-duty housewives, husbands released from offices, shops and factories, and children granted a late reprieve from bedtime, were enjoying the thrilling spectacle of murder on celluloid in an unobtrusive, red-brick, Liverpool building which had once been a church and was now a suburban cinema. Shots and screams rent the air. The children delightedly sucked their lolly-ices. Their excited elders puffed hard at their cigarettes. This was the real thing ! How right they were—this *was* the real thing, for in a little room away from the packed auditorium a masked man stood with a smoking pistol in his hand.

Downstairs in the staff-room of the cinema, two women employees had heard those shots and had realised that they were no part of the show. Running upstairs to see what was wrong, these two women, together with the cinema fireman, who had also heard the shots, had come face to face with a real-life murderer. A man in brown, with something dark covering the lower part of his face and a brown trilby pulled well down over his eyes, he had hesitated for a moment, and then, waving a gun in his hand, had curtly ordered them to stand back as, brushing rapidly past them, he ran out into the street.

In the manager's office at the top of the spiral staircase they found a scene of horror and chaos. The room was filled with the sharp stench of burnt cordite. The furniture was overturned. The manager and the assistant-manager lay in ever-widening pools of blood, and all about them the night's takings were scattered on the floor.

Before many minutes had elapsed an ambulance was speeding

159

from nearby Sefton General Hospital to Webster Road and had drawn up outside the Cameo Cinema.

The manager, 39-year-old Leonard Thomas, was already dead. In the aseptic fastness of the operating theatre white-gowned surgeons fought a losing battle with death. At 11-15 p.m. the other man, John Bernard Catterall, died. Somewhere in the night their killer prowled the concrete jungle of the streets.

The problem facing the Liverpool police was a tough one. Somehow they had to identify and arrest the unknown murderer. They began by questioning those of the cinema staff who had caught a glimpse of the man on the spiral staircase. Their descriptions were necessarily vague. " A man in a belted brown overcoat. Age: 20-30. Height: about 5 feet 7 or 8 inches. Build: medium to broad." That was all. Not much to go on in a city of nearly 800,000 inhabitants. But there *was* one other thing. Something that neither the mask nor the turned-down hat could hide. All the witnesses agreed that the killer had a pair of extraordinarily dark eyebrows.

Later that night, down at the city's Dale Street police head-quarters, Chief-Superintendent Tom Smith, head of the C.I.D., sent for his right-hand man, Chief Detective-Inspector H. R. Balmer. Together they studied the slender description of the wanted man. Then they went along to the criminal record department. Hour after hour the two police-officers checked, painstakingly and methodically, through the thousands of photographs and dossiers in the rogues' gallery. By the time the first pale rays of Sunday's dawn were filtering into the grey room they had decided that a certain George Kelly fitted the description. This Kelly was known as a man of violence and *he had extraordinarily dark eyebrows.*

Chief-Inspector Balmer lost no time. At 11-15 that very morning he interviewed George Kelly at the house in Cambridge Street— less than three minutes walk from the Cameo Cinema—where he was living with a woman named Doris O'Malley. But Kelly had an alibi that was to take the police 327 days to break.

" I was with James Skelly at the Coach and Horses pub just after opening time last night," said a self-confident Kelly. " He was on the booze so I left him and arranged to see him down town. He didn't turn up so I went back at 9 o'clock and saw he was drunk. I jumped a tram to the public-house opposite our street in Picton Road (the Leigh Arms) and stayed there until 10 o'clock, when I came home."

Chief-Inspector Balmer was quick to notice that although his visit was paid at a time when Kelly was usually in bed, he was not only up, but he was also dressed—and dressed fastidiously. It was obvious to him that his arrival had not been altogether unexpected. Without any hesitation, Kelly accompanied him as he set to work to check his alibi, and insisted on being present when James Skelly was interviewed. He was not present, however, when, later that day,

Chief-Inspector Balmer made certain other inquiries which confirmed his suspicion that the story Kelly told of his movements was a false one. But it is one thing to know that an alibi is a fake, proving it to be so is a totally different matter, and at that stage nobody would talk. Georgie Kelly was too well known to " take liberties with."

Well that was, for the time being at any rate, a stop card. During the next six months the police visited 9,500 houses within a square mile of the Cameo Cinema, interviewed 75,000 people and seized 30 revolvers, 3 rifles and a shot-gun. The manhunt was the greatest Merseyside had ever seen, but it was utterly unproductive.

The real turning point in the case came on April 4th, 1949, when an anonymous letter was delivered to Chief-Superintendent Smith. The letter was written in carefully-printed block capitals. " Dear Sir," it began, " this letter is not a crank's letter or such like, nor am I turning informer for gain. You have been searching Wavertree and district for the persons responsible for the death of two men killed in the cinema when the persons responsible live nowhere near where the crime was committed. It says in the papers you are looking for one man. I know three and a girl, not including myself, who heard about this plan for the robbery."

The anonymous correspondent went on to say that two men had gone to the Cameo Cinema on that fatal night, and that, under certain conditions, he was prepared to name them. " If I give my address, you may charge me with being an accessory to the killing. If you put in the personal column of the *Echo* and give me your word that I won't be charged, I will give you both their names."

After due deliberation Chief-Superintendent Smith decided to accept the writer's conditions, and at the head of the personal column of that night's *Liverpool Echo* there appeared the enigmatic insertion " Anonymous letter received. Promise definitely given."

Weeks went by and no reply was received. Meanwhile, handwriting experts decided that the letter had been written by a woman. Night after night, bands of detectives tramped the streets of Liverpool obtaining samples of handwriting from women and girls who had been convicted or were the known associates of criminals. The search dragged on for months. Spring and summer passed, and then, as the dark nights of autumn approached, the police's persistent efforts bore fruit. One night a woman was seen, a woman whose journeyings took her all over the country. The vital question was asked and she answered that she had written the letter. What was more important, she proved that she was speaking the truth by referring to a red smudge of lipstick on the envelope. The search was over, thought the detectives—but they exulted too soon. Almost immediately, the woman disappeared again. Balmer spent weeks in Soho and other parts of London, in Bristol, Birmingham and many more big cities vainly hunting for her. It was not until late September that he traced her to Manchester and she returned with him to Liverpool. This time she did not run away, but made the statement which, together with that of her male companion, was to put the final knot in the noose around George Kelly's bull neck.

The story that Jacqueline Dickson and James ' Stutty ' Northam told was a strange one. At 7-55 on the evening of March 19th, 1949, they had met Kelly and another man, named Charles Connolly, in the Beehive public-house at the bottom of Mount Pleasant. They had some drinks there and began to talk together about possible jobs.

The man Connolly spoke of premises in Islington, but the idea of breaking into them was abandoned because someone mentioned that an automatic burglar alarm was installed there. Kelly then said it might be worth trying to break into a booth at New Brighton fairground, but this was also rejected along with Connolly's proposal that they should rob a taxi driver. It was Connolly who suggested the Cameo Cinema, adding that it would have to be a stick-up job and that a gun would be needed. At this, Kelly drew a revolver out of his hip pocket. On seeing the weapon, Northam and Dickson refused to have anything to do with the robbery and, at about 8-30, after borrowing a hat and overcoat from Northam and a small brown apron to serve as a mask from a second, unnamed, woman, Kelly and Connolly caught a number 8 tram in the direction of Wavertree.

At 1 o'clock the following day the four of them met by appointment at the White Star public-house at the corner of Clarence Street and Brownlow Hill. At that meeting Kelly told Northam and Dickson that it was he who had shot Thomas and Catterall, and that Connolly, who had remained outside in the street keeping watch, had run off and left him when he heard the shooting. He also said that he was not at all worried and had a " cast-iron alibi."

Listening to the amazingly detailed account of the robbery and killings which Northam said Kelly had given him, the police knew that the time had come to pounce and, accordingly, on September 30th, George Kelly and Charles Connolly were arrested.

Kelly adopted an arrogant attitude of outraged innocence and kept on saying that he had a cast-iron alibi. Connolly contented himself with strenuous denials. He did not know George Kelly. He had never been in the Beehive. Anyway, at 9-30 on the evening of March 19th he was at a dance in St. Mark's Church Hall, Edge Lane.

The Cameo Murder Trial opened at St. George's Hall on January 12th, 1950, before Mr. Justice Oliver. For thirteen drama-packed days a long procession of 68 witnesses gave their evidence before a court that was crowded to capacity. Gradually the pieces fitted together. The whole sordid story took shape. The prosecution shattered Kelly's cast-iron alibi into a thousand fragments. And then, on the thirteenth and final day of the longest murder trial in British criminal history . . . the jury disagreed. After an absence of 4 hours and 8 minutes the foreman admitted that there was no hope of their reaching agreement, and the judge had no option but to order a re-trial.

But for Connolly at least, the ordeal was over, for when the second trial opened before Mr. Justice Cassels on February 2nd, 1950, Kelly stood alone in the dock. Charles Connolly had elected to plead guilty to a charge of robbery, in respect of which he was sentenced, on February 13th, 1950, to ten years' imprisonment.

Kelly's second trial lasted six days. This time the jury was not divided. They were out a mere 55 minutes before returning an uncompromising ' Guilty.'

On March 28th, 1950, just one year and nine days after he had brutally murdered two men in a suburban cinema, George Kelly paid with his own life on the scaffold at Walton Gaol. He was only twenty-seven when he died, but his career had been an evil one. From small beginnings in crime when, at the age of eleven, he had been put on probation for school-breaking and larceny, he had graduated through a number of petty offences to his first taste of prison. That was in December 1943 when he received nine months for kicking a pregnant woman in the stomach and rupturing her bladder. Oddly enough, the judge who sent him to prison on that occasion was Mr. Justice Cassels who was later to sentence him to death. His war record was equally unsavoury. On September 28th, 1945, he was discharged from the Royal Navy and sentenced by a court-martial to three years' penal servitude in respect of five charges of desertion.

It was in the slightly feverish atmosphere of post-war Liverpool, however, that Kelly really blossomed forth. He was a little man who loved to act big, and when he was not helping his mother to hawk fruit on her barrow, or acting as barker to the escapologist on the blitzed site at the corner of Ranelagh Street, he liked to make a big splash in the small drinking-pools of the town. " My name's Kelly," he used to boast. " Nobody takes liberties with Kelly." I met him myself and had a glass or two of beer with him. I found him quite amiable, but in the bars and cafés under the bright lights of Lime Street he was a force to be reckoned with. They used to call him the Little Cæsar of Lime Street and, surrounded by his fawning mob of strongarm boys, he saw himself as the sleek well-dressed gang boss of the screen. When he planned the big armed robbery that was to justify himself in his own eyes, it was pathetically in character that he should choose a tiny suburban cinema—and make a hash even of that. Still, he got his little hour of fame in the end, and the man who loved to impress had an audience of more than a thousand people waiting in the street outside St. George's Hall to hear that he had been condemned to death.

Before he passed the extreme sentence of the law, the judge told Kelly, " A man who uses a gun to assist him in a robbery can expect no mercy," and it was not only to the ashen-faced figure in the dock that those words were addressed. They were meant also for the ears of all the spivs and wide boys who might fancy their chances with a pistol. That they found their mark is amply proved by the fact that all this happened seven years ago and from that time to this Liverpool has not had a single case of robbery in which firearms have been used.

AN acquisitive wayfarer discovers,
among other things, a poet-cobbler,
a wounded warrior, the childhood
home of Nicholas ' Cruel Sea '
Monsarrat and a thousand-year-old
oak in the place of the alders.

AFOOT IN ALLERTON

A LLERTON, the place of the alders.
Allerton, where pert pebble-dash rubs shoulders with solid
sandstone in a democratic design for living.

Did I say ' democratic ' ? Well, I don't know that that is quite
the right word, for during my recent wanderings I found a core of
die-hard Allertonians who, ever since the building of the Springwood
Estate, thirty odd years ago, have decided to move themselves over the
border into Mossley Hill. Again and again I met people who indig-
nantly told me : " We do NOT live in Allerton. We are just inside the
boundary of Mossley Hill." Apparently, to have " Mossley Hill " on
your visiting-card lends a distinct cachet hereabouts.

This whole question of boundaries is a vexed one, and when I
tried to sort out exactly where Mossley Hill ends and Allerton begins
I soon found myself in great difficulties. As I was walking up Green
Lane I came upon what looked like an ancient boundary stone, set in a
plot of grass opposite Silverbeech Avenue. And that, according to
local historian Mr. Rupert Finch, is precisely what it is. " But," he
added sadly, " I'm afraid it's been moved from its original position."
Unfortunately, this applies also to the Calder Stones which, in 1578,
were cited as an undisputed boundary point during a territorial
disagreement between the Manors of Allerton and Wavertree. They
were moved from their original site in 1815, and have since been
removed altogether for local archaeologist Mr. J. L. Forde-Johnston to
set about cleaning them with a toothbrush ! So to-day, not only has
the ancient boundary point been lost, but Allerton has also lost the
stones themselves, and with them its title to the claim of harbouring
the oldest examples of man's handiwork on Merseyside—some 4,000-
year-old carvings.

You will still find, however, in Calderstones Park the oldest tree
in Liverpool. Gnarled like an immensely old man, Allerton Oak leans

the weight of a thousand years upon the crutches of a number of iron stays, and tradition whispers that it was beneath those venerable branches that the Hundred Court of Allerton used to meet ten centuries ago.

And within a stone's throw of this sylvan Methuselah is Calderstone House where Charles and Henry MacIver installed the first telephone in actual daily use in or around Liverpool. It is interesting to note that Allerton maintained its traditional progressiveness in the speedy adoption of novel inventions when, in 1948, Mr. I. C. Jones pioneered the first public television demonstrations in Liverpool in a small shop in Allerton Road. Since then Mr. Jones's shop has blossomed into a vest-pocket Olympia where every day you can see twenty-eight television sets functioning simultaneously. Surely so ambitious a venture is unique in any suburb.

★   ★   ★   ★

From 4,000-year-old stone-carvings to the last word in television equipment, that in a way gives you the key to the theme of Allerton. The old and the new side by side. The Allerton Gaumont stands on the site of an old slaughterhouse and its patrons sit in the plush two-and-fours where for 300 years were only shippons and pigsties. And next door to this modern picture-palace the old sandstone farmhouse still survives. Mr. Norman Herd has succeeded farmer Willie Capstick as its tenant, and he told me that, although he keeps a few pigs, there are no longer any cows at the farm, and all the milk that he sells in his dairy comes to him already bottled.

Within living memory little more than a village street, nowadays Allerton Road is a busy shopping thoroughfare, and yet somehow it manages to preserve, in parts, the air of a village. The shopkeepers know all their customers and greet them with a friendly old-world courtesy which surely dates back to the days when the cornfields blew along Menlove Avenue.

And, like a village, Allerton Road has its characters. Chief among these is 67-year-old Mr. William Griffiths, the busy bootmaker. One guesses from his name that Bill Griffiths may count among his ancestors Welsh bards, and some strain of their wild Celtic music must sing in his blood, for Mr. Griffiths is a poet. For many years he has been trying, without much success, to get his poems into print, and so, within the last couple of years, he has taken to publishing them himself. No ordinary man, the poet-cobbler, who sews not a dream but a poem in every seam, scorns such mundane media as paper and printer's ink. Instead, he chalks his verses upon the window of his shop for all who pass to see. Many of the poems have been set to music and on the day I visited him Bill Griffiths had written on his window :

" HERE IS A LOVELY SONG.   Verse 3/4 time.
THE RIVER OF GOLDEN DREAMS
Words and music by
W. GRIFFITHS."

Maybe Mr. Griffiths makes songs and shoes to set people's feet a'dancing, but it is charming Miss Grace Johnson who teaches them *how* to dance. Grace is the daughter of Mr. and Mrs. A. Vernon Johnson, who were so well-known in the dancing years of the 'twenties, and she is still running the dancing school which they opened on Armistice Day, 1918. It was a great success from the start, and to-day many of the sons and daughters of the little boys and girls who were its first pupils are following in their parents' dancing steps. I went into a large studio where a dozen little girls in red tunics were doing natural movements and mimes to the words and music of *The Teddy Bears' Picnic*. Here, the children were not only learning how to dance, they were also being taught self-confidence. A tiny 3-year-old who had been at the school several weeks lisped and mimed *Little Bo-Peep* for me with all the assurance of a veteran, but a shy newcomer wouldn't even enter the studio because, " There's a funny man in there " !

Two of the liveliest people that I met in Allerton were Mr. and Mrs. Joseph Russell who run a little milk-bar that is the teenage social centre of the district. Mrs. Russell, a very vivacious personality, is an old trouper who has performed on stage, radio and television, and lovers of the music-hall will know her best as Helen Trix Lewis. " Running a milk-bar is a bit of a change from life on the boards," she said with a far-away look in her eyes, " but we are always meeting new people and I just love people." " We get lots of college boys and girls in here," chimed in her husband, "and it helps to keep us young in heart."

Young in heart, that certainly describes the Russells and that is also what I would call Mr. Isaac Griffiths. Old Ike wouldn't tell me his age, but he did admit that he is the oldest farmer in Allerton, and West Farm where he lives is one of the last two farms in the district. Across the years Ike Griffiths has seen many, many changes in Allerton. " I used to farm right up Greenhill Road to the parish church," he told me. " A hundred and fifty-four acres. But gradually the land has gone for housing." And he remembers young Nicholas Monsarrat who, long before he rocketed to fame as author of the best-selling novel, *The Cruel Sea*, used to live at Melbreck House off Greenhill Road. I had a look around for Melbreck House, but I learned that the " big, old-fashioned rambling house, with a large garden . . . long corridors, big wide staircases and at least twenty rooms . . ." was no more. Its site is covered now by a trim colony of modern houses, but I did find some of Melbreck's floorboards being used as a hen-pen by Mr. Ernest Wilson at his nursery in Greenhill

Road. " I mind the time," said old Ike, " when it was an event to see a policeman in Allerton." Times certainly have changed in that respect, for now every policeman—and policewoman—in Liverpool has to pass through Allerton's magnificent Police Training School on Mather Avenue.

★   ★   ★   ★

I paid a visit to the school which, opened in 1939 to replace the old premises at Everton Terrace, is the most modern police-force training establishment in the country. It is a clean new-smelling building, very much more cheerful than some of our dim old-fashioned bridewells. In the entrance hall was a glass case filled with silver cups and trophies which had been won by the Force. They were displayed to great advantage against a lovely blue silk banner of the Central Division of the Cuban Police which had been presented by them to the Chief Constable of Liverpool. There, too, was a simple Roll of Honour, set in a carved wood war memorial which was designed and constructed by Detective-Sergeant Norman Ponsford, who has since retired on pension and been ordained a clergyman of the Church of England. And all around, in bright airy class-rooms young men and women were learning how to take and classify finger-prints, how to search scientifically the scenes of crimes, the intricacies of police law and local procedure, and the principles of first-aid. Apart from a floating population of those attending specific courses, there is, too, provision here for a hundred resident cadets between the ages of 16 and 18 who, in two or three years, are taught the basis of police work in the only scheme of its kind in existence in the country.

On the far side of the school playing-fields is the headquarters of the Mounted Department of the Liverpool City Police. A smell of saddle-soap pervades the building. Everywhere are reminders of horses. A pair of riding-boots on the top of a cupboard. A horse's harness beside the typewriter on a desk. I was shown over the stables where the twenty-one chestnut and half-dozen grey horses are kept. What particularly struck me was the amazing cleanliness of everything. There was barely a wisp of straw to be seen in the stable-yard. It was in the stables that I was introduced to 17-year-old Colin, probably the best-known police-horse in Great Britain, who has won every possible cup except the King George V Champion Challenge Cup. Still, Gorey Lad brought that coveted award home to Liverpool from the Richmond Horse Show so nobody is particularly worried about Colin's failure.

And if you think the stables are clean you should see the saddle-room. The floor is polished smooth as ice, the saddles, head-chains, sabres and belts that hang around the walls shine like mirrors. This is the place where the drums that are used in the famous musical ride are kept, and there they are in the centre of the floor, displayed, together with the trumpets, trophies and ceremonial cavalry swords, against a background of crossed lances and pennants.

After that I went to see the kennels where thirty-one Alsatians are being trained to play their part in the battle against a city's crime. The sergeant in charge is an Alsatian enthusiast. He has a couple of his own at home and believes that the Alsatian is the cleverest of all dogs. " I'll guarantee to train one to do anything," he confided. And judging by some of the things that I saw the dogs do as he put them through their paces for me, I don't think that that was an idle boast.

Alsatians were in evidence, too, at Mr. Sam Brown's. Mr. Brown keeps what I think you might call Allerton's Animal Farm at ' Maycot,' Greenhill Road. You can board any pet out here from a cobra to a cavy. " We never refuse any animal," explained Mr. Brown. " Cats, canaries, dogs, polecats, snakes, lizards, goldfish, tortoises, rabbits, budgerigars and monkeys—we've had them all." Once, Mr. Brown was asked to take in a couple of bears. That he had to refuse has been a lifelong grief to him. " But," he told me sadly, " I had no wall stout enough to take the bars of a suitable cage."

★   ★   ★   ★

It was not, however, at Mr. Brown's, but in a small house in Greenhill Road that I found a specimen of the British lion.

Seventy-eight-year-old Lieutenant-Colonel Donald Dickson Farmer, V.C., lives at number 165. It was on December 13th, 1900, that young Sergeant Farmer, who was serving with the Queen's Own Cameron Highlanders in the Western Transvaal, awoke to find his camp surrounded by the Boers. During the fight which ensued an officer was badly wounded, and Sergeant Farmer carried the stricken lieutenant to safety through the firing-line, returning afterwards, at considerable risk, with a supply of much-needed ammunition for his comrades. These outstanding twin gallantries brought him a well-deserved V.C. To-day, the old lion is maimed, for his eyesight is rapidly failing and blindness threatens, but he still has the clear bright eyes of Helen, the Scots lass that he met on Edinburgh's Waverley Station and married 53 years ago, to watch over his welfare. The officer whose life he saved was best man at Colonel Farmer's wedding and he is still alive to-day. He is now eighty years of age and a Major-General. His name is J. V. Sandilands.

I left the Colonel and his lady by their fireside and went in search of the Reverend Robert Martineau, vicar of Allerton. Mr. Martineau, the great, great-nephew of Dr. James Martineau, famous first minister of Hope Street Unitarian Church, is an astronomer, mathematician and botanist of some distinction. He spent a couple of years in South Africa with the R.A.F. and contrived during that time to write the only standard work on Rhodesian wild flowers. When I arrived the vicar was in the throes of moving. He is leaving the old vicarage where for eighty years the vicars of Allerton have lived, and going to a small modern house beside his church. " I shan't be sorry to go," he said. " We have three children and my wife finds it terribly hard work to run such a rambling place as this with only a daily help. Besides, in these days I think it is more fitting that a parson should live in a house which is comparable in size with that of his average parishioner."

★   ★   ★   ★

Since, in 1913, Allerton was taken into the city of Liverpool, many changes have come to it. Well within living memory it has grown from a quiet place of farms and a few mellow sandstone houses into a prosperous green belt suburb. The smell of the cowsheds has faded. Even the rattle of the trams, lurching along silver rails which stretch lengthening steel claws into the heart of the whilom country, is silenced. Doubtless, in the years to come many more changes will be wrought in the name of progress, but the charm of Allerton is such that I do not think any of us need fear to see it fade.

*A HEAT-WAVE day of
dalliance amidst the lotus-eaters
of the sands.*

BESIDE THE SEASIDE

WHEN, the other day, the northern sun peeped coyly from the curtain of cloud behind which it has been sulking for so much of this sullen summer, I, along with what appeared to be the greater part of the population of Liverpool, decided to turn my back upon the breathless city streets and hie me to the riverside playground of New Brighton.

Under a rare blue sky the landing-stage was a colourful bustle of hundreds of compact little family units. There they stood by the shimmering waterside in vast orderly queues, mother, looking five years younger in a gay print frock, father, conceding with open-necked shirt to the spirit of the occasion, and the children bright-eyed and boisterous.

" You've 'ad it, you 'ave," said one harassed mother dragging a tearful five-year-old up the gangway onto the ferry-boat, while grandma, black and boiled in a heavy winter coat, nodded agreement in the background.

The bell on the bridge clanged ; the gangways went up ; ropes were cast off and, amidst the excited chatter of the children, the *Leasowe* shivered into life and nosed gently out into the Mersey. Mother and her brood of little ones settled down in the sunlight on deck to enjoy the twenty-minute voyage, while father stole softly away to the bar to savour the great privilege of a glass of ale out of hours which the law extends to even such ephemeral seafarers.

And before you had had the opportunity to say " Cheers ! " a couple of times, there we were alongside New Brighton, with the whole golden afternoon stretching, like the sands, thirstily before us.

*   *   *   *

Resisting the mute appeal of a pile of deck-chairs, one of which becomes yours for three hours for 6d., and ignoring the notice beside them, " Tide Going Out "—the reverse side of which read " Tide Out All Day " (apparently the deck-chair vendor does not recognise even the possibility of the tide coming in)—I set off to explore the promenade.

On and on I walked—thinking of those vacant deck-chairs—past the little stalls displaying plastic noses, false moustaches, buckets and spades, racks of those traditionally comic postcards showing immensely fat ladies in what always seem to me singularly humourless contexts, and paper hats bearing on their crowns such invitations as " Kiss Me " or " Hug Me Tight."

I hovered uncertainly over trays of gritty molluscs—" They're all fresh. Lovely with a dash of vinegar, sir."—and found myself wondering what kind of people buy hot-dogs and Bovril on so sticky an afternoon. I noticed, too, that shining ice-cream vans have taken the place of the old hokey-pokey man—" Hokey-pokey a penny a lump, that's the stuff to make you jump," his cry, last heard twenty odd years ago, still sounds in my memory.

At length I came to the fair-ground. " Guess your weight ?" asked a man in a short white coat. I nodded. He felt my arms and shoulders. " Twelve stone two," he said. The pointer shot round to 13 stone 5 lbs. He gave me my money back. It was a small compensation.

A coloured man in a brilliant yellow turban wanted to read my hand. I said I would prefer not to know what the future was preparing to spring upon me and went instead into the Tower Museum. It was beautifully cool inside and I discovered among other things a pony-carriage used by Queen Victoria, the Duke of Westminster's perambulator and a magnificent gilt-framed picture constructed entirely of butterflies. It took twenty years to make, and our indigenous lepidoptera was depleted to the extent of 9,000 individuals in the fair cause of art. There was also a machine of the type which reveals the terrible secrets of what the butler saw, only in this case your penny purchases a dozen interesting glimpses of old photographs of the 1914-18 war. From there I graduated to the waxworks where I spent some time in the company of such notables as Ruxon, Christie, Haigh, Landru and Sweeney Todd, the latter depicted in the very act of providing the raw material, as it were, for a batch of Mrs. Lovatt's pies.

*   *   *   *

Escaped once more into the daylight, I shattered my nerves still further by watching an intrepid 17-year-old girl ride the Wall of Death on a noisy bucking motor-bike, and by braving the terrors of the Ghost Train. After that I had recourse to the peaceful panacea of the Tunnel of Love. The young man in charge was an Irishman and, true to pattern, told me, " For every hundred that come, we get eighty schoolchildren." By the time I left the fair it was getting late and the slanting reddish-gold rays of the westering sun were making long shadows on the pier where a few elderly couples sat reading in deck-chairs beside the shuttered bandstand. Borne on a slight breeze, came the far-away music and rumble of the fair. The beach was practically deserted, littered with the trippers' legacy of paper, ice-cream cartons and empty cigarette packets. You could actually hear the waves there—something you had not been able to do all day—as evening came creeping up over the Mersey and along the water's edge in a deep blue shadow of haze.

*　*　*　*

Back aboard the *Leasowe* tired children and sun-pinked parents ate the last sandwiches from brown paper carrier bags. In contrast to our outward bound progress, everyone seemed curiously quiet. Almost the only sound as we drew near to the Pier Head was the lapping of the water and the screaming of the gulls that wheeled about the ship like wind-tossed fragments of white paper. And below in the bar father downed a ruminative glass of stout that had somehow lost its tang because by now " they were open " in Liverpool anyway.

*A BLAMELESS afternoon spent
in contemplation of one of those
bloodless battles which are forever
being fought on the summer
fields of England.*

CRICKET ON THE GREEN

ON a lazy August afternoon you will find at Sefton Park the
nearest thing in Liverpool to cricket on the village green.

Not that I am much of an expert on the game. In my school-
days, when Larwood was petrifying the ' Aussies,' I rather fancied
myself as a body-line bowler, but unfortunately nobody else in the
school eleven shared my enthusiasm. Cricket should be in my blood,
for my mother was one of the best wickets that Huyton College ever
boasted, but to-day my interest is confined to the observing of the
ritual on the green rather than playing any active part in it.

I like to take my ease beside the billiard-table-smooth pitch
and watch the swan-like flight of batsmen, the faint smack of leather
and willow floating to my ears on summer zephyrs.

This afternoon I dreamed away an hour vainly trying to capture
in words the sound of bat meeting ball. It is incredibly difficult.
Even that master manipulator of onomatopoeia, James Joyce, could
get no closer than a totally inadequate " pick, pack, pock, puck : like
drops of water in a fountain falling softly in the brimming bowl."

*   *   *   *

How cool and pleasant it was under the sunshades and under
the trees, feeling faintly guilty at one's own indolence as the sweating
flannelled figures fled the ball about the field, and echoing Mole's
sentiment in *The Wind in the Willows* that " after all, the best part of
a holiday is perhaps not so much to be resting yourself, as to see all
the other fellows working."

And, game or no game, cricket can be very hard work.

Under a grass-withering sun, the brick-faced batsmen struggled
to keep up their ends and, white-coated and bronze-skinned, the
umpire wilted beneath his drape of pullovers.

The bowler walked back what seemed a needless distance from the crease, braced himself, carefully adjusted his fingers about the ball in his hand. Faster and faster he ran, and then, with a grunt, clearly audible from where I sat, he hurled the red leather swift and true upon the middle stump. The batsman made a tremendous swipe, like an angry man trying to swat a wasp, but he was stung—there was a crack as the ball uprooted the stump and the bails flew into the air. A ripple of genteel applause crept languidly around the field.

The vanquished one strolled sedately off, bat tucked under arm, raising his cap to a lady friend as he passed, and everyone settled down to that waiting which plays so prominent a part in all cricket matches.

Throughout the long afternoon the runs piled up on the scoreboard. Bald heads, burned brown, moved from side to side : sharp eyes peered from behind the blue-tinted veils of sun glasses. There were perhaps 2,500 people anxiously following the fortunes of Sefton and New Brighton cricket clubs. Old men sat quietly in the sun remembering the days when they were lissome on the field. Wives, keen-seeming as their husbands, lent their voices to the throaty roars that followed the ball soaring beyond the boundary. And the children jumped up and down in excitement. " Dad, I want to be a cricketer when I grow up," said a rosy-cheeked boy, lip-lined with ice-cream.

★   ★   ★   ★

At five minutes past five came the tea interval, and at a long trestle-table, covered with a snow-white cloth and set with twenty-two bone-china cups and saucers, the players sat down to salad sandwiches and fruit-cake in the pavilion, while W. G. Grace, the cricketer's patron saint, who was in his prime when that pavilion was built, gazed beaverishly down at them from the wall.

By half past five the battle was on again, and tension mounted as the sun sank west. A couple of hours after that and it was all over. Sefton had won a decisive victory—215 for 9, declared : New Brighton, 162. Stumps were drawn ; the crowds dispersed and the players hurried from shower and changing-room to the bar where the last rites of such delightful days are always traditionally performed.

YELLOW, white, red, green and blue, plain, squared and striped, they dribble their way to victory or defeat, and then go home to mark the fortunes of others on the field.

SATURDAY-AFTERNOON GLADIATORS

AUTUMN has come with armfuls of dead leaves and a flurry of football-booted feet, and nowhere is its advent more apparent than on the Saturday-afternoon sports fields of the parks, where the scene has changed from one of cool cricketers in white, languid-seeming beneath blue skies, to a brilliant panorama of flushed men in gaudy shirts chasing the yellow ball between the crisp lines of new-marked pitches, across turf as yet unpitted into a morass of mud by hundreds of stampeding studs.

The placid, pullovered umpire is vanished, and in his place the referee, a tall thin man who looks as if he has a stomach-ulcer, sprints feverishly in the wake of the players. He wears wide black shorts and a suit-jacket, and his hair, combed straight back, adheres, flat and oily, to the contours of his skull. And the linesman, " drest in a little brief authority " and his best blue serge, dances up and down the touch-line with the agility of a dervish, his grubby white handkerchief threshing the air. " Yellow throw-in. Kick-out off White boot. Think back`! " he proclaims pontifically.

★   ★   ★   ★

The battle is between the Yellows and the Whites.

The touch-line is crowded with relatives, friends and workmates. The brother of one of the players is explaining the intricacies of the game to his wife. A woman in a shop-new coat, above whose velvet collar a Medusa mass of cork-screw-tight curls snares the eye, she nods appreciatively.

I take up a position behind a group of those old gentlemen who, carrying walking-sticks with handles uncrooked by the damp of goodness knows what seedy lodgings, are always to be seen, like elderly silvans, in autumn parks. There they stand, rapt, beside the pitch, the smoke from the low-burnt bowls of their pipes curling blue on the afternoon air, acrid-smelling as smouldering leaves.

All around leather lungs shout advice.

" Now then, come on 'Arry, you've got a clear run ! "

" Go on lad, don't be afraid of the ball ! "

" Tackle ! TACKLE ! Blimey, what's wrong with that big black-haired one ? "

" Missed it. Cor ! wouldn't you *know* George would miss it ? "

Two of the players are arguing.

" Listen Ginger, when you're a full-back you're a full-back not a bloody centre-forward."

*   *   *   *

The Whites get the ball and sweep down the field. From boot to boot and head to bullet head, it passes to the danger zone of the Yellow goal—at least I think it is the Yellow goal, but both goal-keepers are dressed like identical twins and I can never tell the difference—and then, just as it seems inevitable that the Whites will score, Ginger charges like an angry black-and-yellow wasp. There is a thud, and the ball soars high into the dull sky.

Ginger, wreathed in smiles, acknowledges the plaudits of the crowd, but the man he has just charged is limping and hopping in very prescribed circles. A man in a flat cloth cap and a pair of green corduroy trousers dashes onto the field with a square wooden first-aid case with the name of the team neatly painted in white upon its lid.

" What's the trouble, Jack ? " There is a tinge of unmalicious hope in his voice.

" Give my leg a rub for us will you, Bill," gasps the injured one.

A momentary flicker of disappointment crosses Bill's face. One has the feeling that he was ready for anything. On the slightest provocation he would have produced a rusty penknife and performed an amputation there and then. As it is, he falls to his knees, opens his little case, extracts a pot of wintergreen-smelling ointment and begins to massage Jack's thigh with a willing vigour which surely compensates for any lack of skill.

*   *   *   *

Now, Saturday afternoon is dying. There is a greyness creeping over the treetops ; the grass grows dusky. At five o'clock the whistles blow and all over the huge field goal-posts are pulled up. Yellow, white, red, green, blue, plain, squared and striped, the figures dribble off the field and, victors and vanquished, go home to tea and to check the outcome of other games of football against a coupon upon which rather more is at stake.

THE NIGHT THEY TRIED TO BURN LIVERPOOL

May 1st, 1941.

That date belongs to history, for that was the night that history was written in letters of fire across the Mersey sky. It was the night, too, that ushered in what was probably the worst week (up to that time) that the world had ever known.

Sixteen years have gone by since then and still the full story of all the horrors and splendours of those seven soul-shattering nights has not, until now, been told. Sixteen years during which a new generation has grown up that knows nothing of its home-town's terrible ordeal by fire. A generation for whom a blitzed site simply means a conveniently clear stretch of waste land upon which to play a game of football. A generation to whom that ominous gap in a row of terrace houses has no more significance than as a useful short cut to the shops. For these young people the sound of an aircraft passing overhead is part of the pattern of life. Even the rush and scream of a jet evokes no more than the admiring craning of a neck, whereas for those older ones amongst us who lived through the fearful years of Hitler's *blitzkrieg* such innocent sounds vibrate deep chords of memory and, just for a split second, fire-bright pictures come crowding into our minds.

May 1st, 1941, was a Thursday, and shortly before 11 p.m., just as the men and women of Merseyside were preparing to go to bed, the dismal keening of sirens sounded on the still night air. It was a nuisance. Tired workers clambered back into their clothes. Sleepy-eyed children were snatched from their cots. With a shrug, mother put the kettle on. It was going to be another late night. Weary, red-eyed people filed into the shelters. It *was* a nuisance, but folk had grown used to that sort of thing in those days. It seemed to them that it was just another routine raid. What they did not—could not—know was that to-night was different : to-night was to be the fiery prelude to a fugue of fear in seven searing episodes. What they did not—could not—know was that on Hitler's desk in Berlin there lay that night a memo addressed to the Führer by Herr Raeder, and in that memo were the significant words :

> " An early concentrated attack on Britain is necessary, *on Liverpool for example*, so that the whole nation will feel the effect."

This memo was the direct result of the failure of Goering's Luftwaffe to defeat the R.A.F. which, together with certain bickerings which had for some time been taking place between the German Military and Naval High Commands, had led to the continued postponement of the proposed invasion of Britain. Faced now with his Secret Service's warnings of the ill-omened entry of the Soviet Union into the war, and thoroughly frustrated by the lack of effective co-operation between his war leaders, Hitler began seriously to consider Raeder's plan to starve Britain into submission by the cutting of her imports.

Great Britain, being an island, must obviously in time of war rely to a very considerable extent upon the streams of weapons, munitions, raw materials and food-stuffs which flow to her ports across the seas of the world. Paralyse her ports and you effectively cut off her vital supplies. That Liverpool could not be closed to traffic by submarine warfare alone had become apparent early in 1940, and now, growing rapidly more and more desperate, the Führer decided to implement Raeder's suggestion and hurl the full fury of his Luftwaffe into a determined effort to put the Port of Liverpool out of commission.

All of this came to light, of course, after the war, when British and American intelligence officers captured the German naval archives and amongst them the minutes of what were known as the " Führer Conferences," and back in May 1941, neither the British Government nor the man in the shelter had the slightest suspicion that Liverpool was about to become Number One Target.

From the number of planes operating that night—there were about 50 of them—it looked at first as though an exceptionally heavy-scale onslaught might be expected, but, due it is believed to deteriorating weather conditions on the other side of the English Channel, the attack suddenly faded out and the raiders scuttled for home.

The first bomb was dropped on Wallasey at 10-50 p.m., and for some time at the beginning of the raid only the roar of a heavy anti-aircraft barrage could be heard, and the black velvét of the sky was spattered with the sequins of bursting shells.

Then, suddenly, a rain of hundreds of incendiaries began to fall and, between their flickering focuses of fire, the heart-fluttering thud and thump of high-explosive bombs began to tremble the earth.

All in all, that first night was not an outstandingly bad one, judged by the standards of those explosive days. There were rather less than 100 incidents in Liverpool and none at all in Bootle. What damage there was was heavy rather than widespread. Low Hill and Cazneau Street suffered, and the North Market, the roof of which was in process of being repaired after being damaged in a previous raid, was hit again. Batty's Dairy in Arundel Avenue, Sefton Park, was struck. The proprietor, his son and 19 cows were buried under the debris and one cow was blown into the roadway where a policeman ran into it on his bicycle in the darkness.

A bomb which blasted the front from a wholesale tobacconist's provided a passing docker with an opportunity to exercise that ' scouse ' sense of humour which even Hitler's high-explosives never succeeded in demolishing. He looked at the broken relics of thousands of those then rare luxuries and said laconically, " If it's not pubs it's cigarettes Jerry goes for ! "

And there was the usual crop of freak incidents such as the saving of the James family by a piano. The blast from a nearby bomb blew in the front portion of the house, but the family, who were lying in bunks in the dining-room, were protected by the piano in the parlour, which stood against the dividing wall and bore the full brunt of the blast.

A woman's intuition saved the 5-year-old son of a Mr. and Mrs. Hamilton. The boy was sound asleep upstairs and all at once his mother became strangely uneasy. Without a word, she rushed up to his room and carried him downstairs. Almost the moment she re-entered the lounge there came a terrific crash from upstairs. Several large lumps of concrete had come bursting through the bedroom window and smashed the bed where, sixty seconds before, her child had been sleeping.

Not quite so happy is the story of a Mrs. Gladys Cooper and her daughter, also Gladys, who had only recently come to 44 Avondale Road, Sefton Park, after being bombed out of their home in another district of Liverpool. The two women usually sheltered under the stairs, but on this particular night they decided that they would go out into the corporation domestic shelter at the back of the house. Unfortunately, the shelter received a direct hit and they were both killed. The house was also severely damaged but, by one of those ironic twists of fate, the stairs still stood, and had the Coopers been beneath them as they generally were the odds are that they would have been perfectly safe.

At 1 a.m. the ' All Clear ' sounded and Merseyside went back to bed. There were still several hours to go to dawn, but the sky was already bright with the reflection of the fires. Fires which even now the Fire Service was battling to quell, but some of which would still be burning to-morrow night, pointing red fingers along the bombing run to what the communiqués called " a North-Western Port," when for the second successive night the Luftwaffe came to try to crush the brave heart of Liverpool.

BACKGROUND TO A BLITZ

IN order properly to appreciate Merseyside's outstanding achievement in the face of its seven-night trial by fire, it is necessary to know something of the nine months preceding that catastrophic week—nine months during which the people of " a North-Western Port " learned by bitter experience the lessons which enabled them to carry on under a vicious bombardment.

For Merseyside the Battle of Britain began on the night of August 8th-9th, 1940, but prior to that there had been the wailing voice of the siren and the stomach-turning thuds of a few bombs. Actually, Merseyside's first alert was sounded on June 25th, 1940, and it was on that day, too, that the heavy double-noted throb that we were to come to know so well first droned from behind the low-hanging clouds. People ran to their dugouts and shelters. Civil defence personnel grabbed their tin hats and dashed to their action stations. Anti-aircraft crews took up watchful positions behind guns whose black mouth-gaps pointed hungrily at the sky. But . . . nothing happened. No bombs. No gunfire. The muttering of Goering's dark angels died away in the distance. The ' All Clear ' sang out and, feeling perhaps a little foolish, everyone took up the threads of their normal lives where they had so abruptly dropped them.

It was during the following month that the bombs first dropped— three of them by a searchlight post at Altcar on the night of July 28th, and, about the same time, several more at Thurstaston, Irby and Neston. They fell in fields and did no particular damage, but the deep craters which they dug drew crowds of sightseers.

But it was as a string of six heavy bombs screamed earthwards at Prenton, Birkenhead, at 12-30 a.m. on that night of August 8th-9th, 1940, that Merseyside's battle really began with the spilling of the first blood.

The first of those bombs fell in the garden of the house of Captain Alan Layfield, commandant of the Special Police, who was on duty in Birkenhead Town Hall at the time. His wife and three other people had narrow escapes. The second bomb, however, scored a direct hit, striking the roof of Mr. and Mrs. W. Bunney's home, a few hundred yards away in Prenton Lane. In an upstairs room in that house a 34-year-old domestic servant lay asleep. She was killed instantly and passed into history as the first of Merseyside's 3,875 victims of the death that fell from the clouds. Her name was Johanna Mandale.

Within twenty-four hours of that first fatal bombing, a stick of seven high-explosives fell on Wallasey, spattering the black earth of a railway embankment, tumbling the bricks of houses at Stroud's Corner, Cliff Road and Mill Lane, and causing 32 casualties. And following close upon the heels of those first attacks on Birkenhead and Wallasey, there came, at midnight on August 17th, the first stick of bombs on Liverpool itself. Residents in the Caryl Street area heard the whistle of the bombs which fell in the Dock Road. The Overhead Railway and a corn silo were damaged, but the nearby tenements escaped. There was no loss of life and only six people were slightly injured.

On August 19th the first incendiary bombs to be dropped in Liverpool fell on the Eaton Road district of West Derby and at Norris Green. At one stage hundreds of them were burning but, fortunately, they mostly landed on open spaces. One, however, struck the Robert Davies Nursing Home, but did little damage.

There was a lull then until August 28th, when a series of spasmodic light attacks was initiated with the loosing of strings of incendiaries on Fulwood Park and Grassendale, and high-explosives on West Derby, Mossley Hill Church and Mersey Road.

In a small-scale raid on August 29th, the centre of the city escaped damage, but Bootle had its first attack and its first bomb —an incendiary—dropped on the gas-works in Hawthorne Road.

The third light raid, on the night of August 30th, saw incendiaries on the Dock Estate and Mill Road Infirmary, and high-explosives on Grafton Street and Brodie Avenue. That night, too, Wallasey High School for Girls was bombed.

On August 31st, however, the Luftwaffe stopped playing with us, and from that date until the end of November, Merseyside had almost continuous raids. The night of the 31st brought a heavy attack. In Liverpool alone there were more than 100 fires, mostly small, and the casualty figures were 23 dead and 86 injured.

In the city centre, Cleveland Square was badly knocked about, and the Custom House was hit and set on fire, while on the outskirts, houses were damaged in the Edge Lane area and fires were started at the Dingle Oil Jetty.

Bootle was again an important target, and at Wallasey the Town hall was wrecked and its £3,500 organ absolutely destroyed.

September 1940, was in the main a month of what may be described as sharp raids. Out of a total of 20 raids Liverpool was bombed 16 times, Birkenhead 11 times, Bootle and Wallasey 9 times each, and Crosby 4 times.

The bombing of the Keilberg Children's Convalescent Home in Birkenhead on September 6th aroused widespread indignation, but happily there were no fatalities among its 30 little occupants. Nevertheless, people were angry. To bomb docks and factories, warehouses and power-stations was one thing, but these constant, indiscriminate attacks on hospitals, churches, schools and a score of other buildings which could not by the wildest stretch of imagination be construed as military objectives, were quite another matter. It got John Bull's goat and many of us sympathised with the emotion which impelled one man to chalk upon his window: " BEWARE HITLER, THERE WILL COME ANOTHER DAY."

On September 18th high-explosives fell on Walton Gaol, partially demolishing one wing and burying captives and captors alike. Twenty-one bodies were taken away by the Mortuary Service. The Governor, however, was adamant that 22 of his prisoners were missing, and did everything short of accusing the service of aiding and abetting an escape. But the mortuary men stuck to their guns and the Governor was finally proved wrong when, eleven years later, the missing body was found beneath some rubble which was being removed from the blitzed wing of the prison.

September 26th was a baddish night with a substantial fire-raising raid on the docks that necessitated the calling in of fire-brigades from Bootle and Birkenhead. That night Birkenhead itself lost its world-famous Argyle Theatre, which was reduced to a mere shell. Other Birkenhead buildings seriously damaged included the Public Assistance Office and the Argyle Street Income Tax Offices.

An entry on the casualty sheet for the last day of September is especially poignant. Despite determined raiding by enemy forces, there was only one fatal casualty in Liverpool that night and beside the man's name are written the words " Caused by shrapnel."

October brought 15 light raids, in which the bombing figures stood at : Liverpool 14 times, Birkenhead 7, Bootle 6, and Wallasey 3.

One of the most terrifying incidents of the entire month occurred on the evening of October 3rd. It was still daylight when a solitary, three-engined, German bomber suddenly swooped on a Liverpool bus. The bus was taking a number of women factory workers home when the conductor shouted to Driver H. O. Smith that a German plane was coming down low behind them. By then the aircraft was practically on their tail and Driver Smith could hear the rattle of its machine-guns. Quick as a flash, he accelerated and swerved to the opposite side of the road. One of the passengers, 17-year-old Lily Gilmore, who was on the upper deck of the bus with her friend, Joan Smith, afterwards described the chase. " We heard the plane first," she said, " and then we could see it clearly diving towards us. We heard a pinging noise and guessed it must be bullets spattering the roof. The driver of the bus went at a great speed and he did marvellously. He had us at a shelter in a very short time. The German plane was still machine-gunning as we raced for the shelter. There was an auxiliary fireman near and we saw his hat knocked off, presumably by a bullet. We saw the funny side of that later."

Though many of the October raids were relatively small affairs, their cumulative effect made a considerable impact on the life of Merseyside. But looking back we see them, and indeed all that went before, as a preparation : a preparation for November, the month in which Merseyside was to have its real baptism of fire.

THE HORROR NIGHT OF LAND-MINES

NOVEMBER 1940, will always be remembered as the month of the horror night of land-mines—November 28th.

These gigantic land-mines, which floated slowly down to earth below green parachutes, were something new, and at first no one knew quite what to make of them.

Indeed, one of the very first to fall caused a certain army sergeant no little embarrassment. This particular sergeant was an enthusiastic, but not especially popular member of his unit, and on the night in question he spotted what he thought was a German airman coming down by parachute. He immediately turned out the guard, and they charged with fixed bayonets.

Just then the moon came out from behind a cloud, and the soldiers saw the sinister shape of a giant land-mine swaying to and fro below its silken 'chute.

Never was the order to retreat given with such feeling or complied with more quickly. And never did an unpopular sergeant have more difficulty in living down an error of judgement.

One of the earliest of these land-mines came down on a mid-Victorian house in a residential quarter of Liverpool. It crashed through the roof and wall at an angle, its nose pointing bluntly into a bedroom. As it was the first unexploded mine ever to fall on the city, a high-ranking officer of the Civil Defence Service decided that he ought to go and have a look at it.

When he arrived at the house he found a naval rating with his ear pressed to the mine, and a young naval officer perched on the top of a rickety pair of steps coolly unscrewing the gain.

" I say, old boy, if this bally thing starts to tick you have precisely ten seconds before she pops," drawled the officer with a nonchalant smile.

" Thank you very much," said the visitor as he tiptoed out into the night !

The month opened in Liverpool with a series of nine lightish raids, which took place between the 1st and the 22nd. The first four raids were not very serious. A number of incendiaries dropped in Great Howard Street, the County Road area, on the East Lancashire Road and at Bowring Park, Huyton and Childwall. High-explosives fell on the junction of Queen's Drive and Townsend Avenue and in Wavertree Playground. The fifth, which lasted from 8 to 9-30 p.m. on the evening of November 12th, was the most violent. There were oil bombs on a post-office in Wavertree Road, high-explosives on Edge Hill Railway Goods Station, and severe damage was done to house property in Edinburgh, Saxony and Albert Edward roads. The death roll amounted to 13, and 18 people were injured. That was the night the B.B.C. came to Liverpool with one of its " They Went To It " programmes, and listeners all over the country heard the singing and chatter of 2,000 people in an underground shelter. Individual shelterers came to the microphone and told how bombs had wrecked their homes, and bus driver H. O. Smith was there to tell his story of the night the German bomber chased his bus. The Commandant of the Auxiliary Fire Service paid tribute to the permanent city fire-brigade, and A.R.P. workers spoke modestly of the work they were doing. The microphones went into the heart of dockland, and also to the Sailors' Home and the Gordon Smith Institute, where men of the mercantile marine service told cheerfully of hardships they had endured. And just to show the rest of the country that in spite of everything Merseyside was not a mournful place, the tour ended at a dance-hall where 1,400 dancers, ignoring the bursts of gunfire that drowned the drums, waltzed and twirled under the coloured lights. The broadcast ended with a message from Liverpool to the capital, " If you can keep it up so can we." And London answered, " We can keep it up all right, and we are proud that you, Liverpool, are doing the same. So stick it, Merseyside, it's worth it."

The following night Wallasey had a raid in which considerable damage was done to corporation property in a number of places, but after that the borough enjoyed a five weeks' lull.

At 7-23 p.m. on the evening of November 28th, the sirens ushered in the 58th attack on Liverpool and, between that time and 4 a.m. the next morning, 150 planes unleashed all the fury of the Luftwaffe in the first really full-scale blitz on the port. This fearsome raid was the second major stroke in the air blockade which had been initiated by a medium-sized attack on Southampton five days previously.

In all the raids up to then Liverpool had suffered a total of 250 deaths. On that night alone, more than 200 people died. The main weight of the attack lasted two and a half hours until 10 o'clock, and hundreds of high-explosive and incendiary bombs, plus 30 huge land-mines (8 of which failed to explode) were unloaded upon the city.

Strangely enough, no incidents were reported from the city centre : that was the night when, in the language of the time, the suburbs " caught it." And catch it they certainly did—Allerton, Childwall, Wavertree and Woolton ; Rose Hill, Edge Hill, Mossley Hill and Garston—despite a " ring of steel " put up by the anti-aircraft guns. Flares dropped by enemy planes made streets as bright as daylight. People in public shelters sang Christmas carols as the bombs whistled down. The blast from a high-explosive damaged one of the stands at the Stanley Greyhound Racing Track, where the kennels were also hit. A number of dogs got loose, but only one was killed and the remainder were soon rounded up. In one house a grandfather-clock, which had been presented to its owner fifty years before, was stopped by a bomb for the first time in half a century. A man whose home was razed owed his life to the fact that that night he had gone to the cinema for the first time in two years. And then there was the Liverpool family that was trapped in a basement and was fed for twenty-four hours on milk which was poured to them down a long steel tube. Undaunted, they used this queer ' food-line ' as a speaking-tube, shouting back messages of encouragement through it to those who were fighting to release them.

What Churchill afterwards described as " the worst single incident of the war " occurred that night when, at 0155 hours, a parachute land-mine demolished the Junior Technical School at Durning Road. There were close on 300 men, women and children taking refuge in a shelter in the basement of that building—people who normally used it, plus many more who had gone there four hours earlier when other shelters in the vicinity were damaged, and the passengers from two trams which had stopped outside it as the raid reached a climax. The land-mine brought the three stories of that solid building toppling down. The shelterers were trapped beneath the wreckage, and to add to the horror the school furnaces, which were situated in the basement, burst, and fire broke out in the debris. A heroine, whose courage must not be allowed to go unsung in any account of that awful disaster, was a middle-aged woman air-raid warden, Mrs. F. B. Taft. She it was who, half-choked by dust and the acrid fumes of smouldering woodwork, and with the level of the water from a burst boiler and a ruptured water-main slowly creeping up, did by her wonderful example prevent a panic. Here is what a husband and wife, two lucky ones who, miraculously, escaped that terrible carnage, had to say of her :

" If anyone deserves a medal it is that woman. She was magnificent in her courage and common-sense. Even as we heard groans from the dying, some of them children, she never cracked up. None of us thought that we would ever get out alive, but Mrs. Taft kept cheering up everyone. When people said, ' We'll never get through,' she just replied, ' They'll get us out all right.' A direct hit was made on the shelter just after my wife and myself had entered. The shelter lights fused, a boiler burst and a fire started at one end. The mass of people made it almost impossible to move about. The roof came through under the enormous weight of the debris and the best we could say was that we believed the victims' end was instantaneous. The horror of it all did not rob people of their courage. None of the women screamed. Nobody fainted. For the first few seconds we did not realise that we had been buried. We tried to scramble for the exits. Mrs. Taft said, ' Keep calm and try the emergency exits.' They were jammed, too. We all thought we were lost. Then, to add to our troubles, a fire started somewhere in the main section. I could see it over the brickwork. It wasn't apparently very large, but smoke poured into our part and people nearly choked with fumes. Water from the burst boiler and the broken water-main slowly flooded the floor of the shelter. It rose to our knees. We didn't know where it was coming from or where it would stop, and wondered if we should be drowned. Then Mrs. Taft shouted, ' I can see a light.' She had found a small window leading out of the shelter which had not been blocked by the terrific amount of debris. She raised a cry for volunteers to dig a way through. Four men came forward. They flashed a torch and someone outside saw it. Rescue work began." Mrs. Taft, her daughter and 3-year-old granddaughter were among those who escaped from the shelter. Doctors and nurses worked side by side with the firemen and rescue parties throughout the night. An auxiliary fireman told how he helped to extricate a little girl of about seven years old. She was trapped beneath two dead adults and could not move an inch. " While we were trying to get her out—and it took an hour or two," he said, " she was quite cheerful and seemed only concerned about her mother who was also trapped." The final casualty figures for Merseyside's most dreadful tragedy were : 164 killed and 96 injured. Between 20 and 30 people out of 290 escaped unharmed. A 24-year-old man was the last living person to be resurrected from that grim tomb. " We were amazed to see the man alive," said a rescue worker. " He had lived for two days in a pocket in the shelter formed by the debris. This pocket in the mass of the masonry had protected him from both fire and water. His first request to us was for a cigarette."

The half-dozen or so scattered bombs which fell in the vicinity of Edge Hill Station on the night of November 29th brought that sad month to a close.

During the past three months Merseyside had had a total of 44 raids, that is an average of one practically every other night. Now there was to be a welcome breathing-space of three weeks of relative peace before Hitler sent the Third Reich's Yuletide greetings to Merseyside.

GLIMPSES through the crystal portals of various Aladdin's caves prompt the drawing forth of some treasured memories from a lengthening stocking.

THE SPIRIT OF CHRISTMAS PAST

IT began, my game of personal charades, or consequences maybe, with a Christmas tree in a window in Upper Parliament Street.

I enjoy taking long, lone strolls at night, and round about Christmas-time they become more interesting because of the sudden gay glimpses of uncurtained cosiness, ballooned, festooned and hollied, which slot the blank faces of the houses with tiny glass-walled Aladdin's caves.

My attention was riveted to this particular tree in this particular window for a very particular reason. Standing there, a voluntary outcast of the streets, I saw—or seemed to see—a small boy peeping from that window. His watching presence was no riddle. I knew what he was doing. His eyes were scanning the empty street for a tram. No ordinary tram this. Not one of those latterday monsters, stream-lined, cream and green, but a ramshackle, buff and maroon Emett contraption with a tin-plate portrait of Mr. Punch affixed to the open wire cage at the front of its top deck. I knew, because, a quarter of a century ago, I was that small boy. I remembered how, on that far-away Christmas eve, crouched in the shadow of an enormous Christmas tree, I had begged my father to extend the privilege of a postponed bedtime just long enough to see one more Mr. Punch.

And the suddenly-evoked memory of that tram set my mind travelling back along the curved track of time where Christmas after Christmas stood out like frosted milestones.

*   *   *   *

The Upper Parliament Street of to-day is a very different place from that which, spick and span and charmingly aligned with tubs of trees, played so great a part in the history of my family and myself.

189

The old house, where Mary, the cook, mixed the Christmas pudding in the vast basement kitchen, still stands, but it is become a rooming-house. The high bedroom where, nose pressed to window-pane—anticipating by many years her son's tram-watching pro-clivities—a little girl awaited breathlessly the Gothic passing splendour of the bejewelled and fairy-lit illuminated tram, is now the one-roomed home of a family of four.

Indeed, all this area is fraught for me with the spirit of Christmas past, for within a stone's throw of Upper Parliament Street, there moulders a house where, a hundred years ago, great-grandfather and his seventeen children observed *Weinachten* with true Germanic veneration. Great-grandfather hailed from Zurich and he was a musician. After introducing quartet music into England, he settled here in Liverpool and, in 1843, became the first conductor of the Liverpool Philharmonic Society's orchestra. Each December he had a huge Christmas tree of the sort which never drops its needles sent to him from Germany. Magnificently decorated and hung with real fruit, it would stand in a locked room until the great day arrived.

Every Christmas eve great-grandfather would don the beard and mantle of Santa Claus. Late at night a thunderous knock would resound through the hushed and expectant house, and Father Christ-mas, together with Tom, his drunken servant, would appear leading a live donkey, complete with present-laden panniers, right into the basement kitchen. Watched by the wide-eyed children, he would march upstairs to the study. There the little ones were interviewed one by one and, producing a magic mirror from beneath his scarlet gown, great-grandfather would look into it and tell each in turn of his or her outstanding misdemeanours during the past year.

The children were all terrified by this annual apparition and the superstitious Irish cook would cross herself and quake with fright. So brilliantly was the whole ceremony acted that even the older children failed to recognise their father. After more than a century the identity of Drunken Tom remains a deep, dark, family mystery.

*　　*　　*　　*

And once set in motion this game of summoning back the past gathered momentum. Christmas after Christmas passed in brilliant panorama across the black canvas of the streets. I remembered cosy Pickwickian Christmases in my grandparents' rambling old house in Mossley Hill. I saw the sudden flames leap orange in the twinkling brass of the morning-room, the snow on the lawn beyond the window. I heard the rustling of presents being unwrapped and saw again with the surprised eyes of childhood the tumbling cornucopia of an up-ended toy-stuffed pillow-case. Picture succeeded picture with the startling effect of those transformation scenes beloved of the Victorians.

It was a sad pleasure, for somewhere along the line the delighted little boy who watched for Mr. Punch in Parliament Street seemed to have got lost.

⋆   ⋆   ⋆   ⋆

It was getting late now. The last of the revellers from the first cautious Christmas parties had gone home. The lights of the Christmas trees in the windows had burned low—gone out. I was suddenly beset with an overwhelming sense of loneliness, and it was this loneliness that brought a last picture back to me.

I saw myself in a strange land. It was Christmas eve and a burning sun blazed in the blue sky of Naples. I was a soldier setting my foot on Italian soil for the first time. As, with my khaki fellows, I made my way to the little village of Lauro, I felt all of that terrible nostalgia for an old-fashioned English Christmas which assails every exile. That night it took formidable quantities of Marsala and *vino*, *bianco* and *rosso*, to blunt the edge of my anguish. And then the miracle—a small miracle—happened. I awoke the next morning to the carillons of many bells. It was Christmas Day, and as I peeped out of my tent I doubted my sight ; the ground, which only a few hours before had been parched and brown with dust, was white with snow. Enchanted Neapolitan snow !

In the evening I was invited to a party at the villa of the local marchesa, an Englishwoman who had married an Italian nobleman, and there, in a room perfumed by the smoke of burning orange-wood, we spent a wonderful and traditionally-English Christmas night.

It was only when the party was over and I found myself walking back alone to camp that the ache and the loneliness returned to my heart.

It was a beautiful night, cold and clear, with a high bright moon silvering the snowy night-caps of the Apennines. My footsteps rang out on the frosted air, a light twinkled somewhere up in the hills, a dog barked in the distance and those self-same stars that must once have shone over a stable in Bethlehem made a diadem on the black brow of the sky.

And before me stretched the road which I knew I must follow. That road was to lead right across Europe. Many Christmases were to pass, knots in a rope of days, before I had travelled its twisting length and it had finally led me—home.

191